WAR CRIMES

BLITZ EDITIONS

Published by Blitz Editions
an imprint of Bookmart Ltd
Registered Number 2372865
Trading as Bookmart Ltd
Desford Road
Enderby
Leicester LE9 5AD

ISBN 1 85605 140 4

This material has previously appeared in *The Encyclopedia of True Crime*.

Every effort has been made to contact the copyright holders for the pictures. In some cases they have been untraceable, for which we offer our apologies. Special thanks to the Hulton-Deutsch Collection, who supplied the majority of pictures, and thanks also to the following libraries and picture agencies: Robert Hunt, Imperial War Museum, Marshall Cavendish, Midsummer Books, Popperfotos, Press Association, Frank Spooner Pictures, Topham

Designed by COOPER WILSON DESIGN

WAR CRIMES

POL POT
The Murder Machine

A gentle nation, ancient in its culture, pious in its faith, was cruelly dismembered by a Marxist fanatic. Pol Pot turned Cambodia into a killing field while the world turned its back on this lost nation.

Above: ***The grinning face of evil – Pol Pot is a study in tyranny and murder. He turned his gentle land into a vast 'killing field'.***

Imagine a government that comes to power, then declares that money is banned. Not only money, but the forces which provide money – commerce, industry, banking – are also proscribed. The new government decrees that society will become agrarian again, just like it had been in the Middle Ages. Great cities and towns will be de-populated and the people will be moved to the countryside, where they will live and work raising crops and cattle. But families will not be allowed to stay together. The government, in its infinite wisdom, realises that children must not be influenced by outdated and archaic bourgois thoughts passed down by their parents. So they are taken away and brought up as the vanguard of the regime, imbued with and steeped in the philosophy of the new order. No messing about with books until they are in the late teens – there is no need for books anymore, so they are burned – and children from the age of seven will begin working for the state.

For the new agrarian class, there are eighteen-hour days, back-breaking work, followed by 're-education' in Marxist-Leninist thought from their new masters. Anyone who dissents, or who shows signs of 'regression' to the old ways is not allowed to live – nor are intellectuals, teachers and college professors; nor those people who are literate because they might read thoughts which are not Marxist-Leninist, and spread a poisonous philosophy among the re-educated workers in the fields. Priests, with their outmoded theology, politicians of any hue other than that of the ruling party and those who made fortunes under previous governments are no longer needed: they too are eliminated. There is no trade, there are no telephones, there are no churches or temples, here are no bicycles, birthday parties, marriages, anniversaries, love or kindness. At best, there is work for the state – torture, degradation and at worst, death.

This nightmare scenario was not a figment of some science fiction writer's imagination. It became a terrible reality in Cambodia, where leader Pol Pot turned the clock back and pushed civilisation out, hoping to find his own warped vision of a classless society. His 'killing fields' were littered with the corpses of those who did not fit into the new world that his brutal

AS MANY AS THREE MILLION PEOPLE MAY HAVE PERISHED DURING POL POT'S REGIME IN CAMBODIA.

Above: ***Leading a column of his faithful followers, Pol Pot treks through the Cambodian jungle.***

subordinates were shaping. As many as three million people may have perished during Pol Pot's regime in Cambodia – the same number of unfortunates killed in the gas chambers of the Auschwitz death factory run by the Nazis in the Second World War. Life under Pol Pot was intolerable and Cambodians were forced to tragically re-christen their South-East Asian country. They gave it the macabre name of the Land of the Walking Dead.

The Cambodian tragedy was a legacy of the Vietnam War that first marked the end of French colonialism before escalating into the conflict against the Americans. Fifty-three thousand Cambodians were slain on the fields of battle. Between 1969 and 1973 American B-52 aircraft carpet-bombed huge tracts of Cambodia, dropping as many tons of high-explosive on the tiny land as had fallen on Germany in the last two years of the Second World War. The Viet Cong fighters in Vietnam used its neighbour's lush jungles as encampments and staging posts for operations against the Americans, and these hideouts were the targets of the war planes.

HE ORDERED THE ABOLITION OF ALL MARKETS, THE DESTRUCTION OF CHURCHES AND THE PERSECUTION OF ALL RELIGIOUS ORDERS.

Prince Norodom Sihanouk, ruler of Cambodia and heir to its great religious and cultural traditions, renounced his royal title ten years before the onset of the Vietnam War, but remained the head of his country. He tried to guide his country along a path of neutrality, a delicate balancing act for a country surrounded by warring states and conflicting ideologies. He had been crowned King of Cambodia, a French protectorate, in 1941, but abdicated in 1955. However, he returned, after free and fair elections, as head of state.

Between 1966 and 1969, as the Vietnam War escalated in intensity, he upset policy-makers in Washington by ignoring the arms smuggling and the Vietnamese guerilla camps in the jungles of Cambodia. At the same time, he was only mildly critical of the punishing air raids being launched by America. On 18 March, 1970, while he was in Moscow, his prime minister, General Lon Nol, with the backing of the White House, staged a coup, after which he changed the name of Cambodia back to its ancient title, Khmer. The Khmer Republic was recognised by the United States, which, however, one month later, chose to launch an invasion against the newly-named land. Sihanouk went into exile in Peking... and here the ex-king chose to form an alliance with the devil himself.

Not much is known about Pol Pot, the man with the fat face and sparkling eyes, the man with the face of an avuncular old grandfather and the heart of a murderous tyrant. He was the monster with whom

Sihanouk threw in his lot, swearing with this Communist guerilla chief that they would mould their forces into a single entity with the aim of destroying American forces. Pot, brought up by a peasant family in the Kampong Thom province of the country, had been educated at a Buddhist monastery where, for two years, he lived as a monk. In the 1950s he won a scholarship to study electronics in Paris where, like so many other students of the time, he became involved in left-wing causes. Here he heard about – although it is unclear whether they actually met – another Cambodian student, Khieu Samphan, a political science student whose controversial but exhilarating plans for an 'agrarian revolution' were to inspire the ambitions of the peasant, Pol Pot.

Above: ***Government troops surround refugees during the Khmer Rouge fighting.***

Top: ***Refugees flee from the city of Phnom Penh.***

POL POT, THE MAN WITH THE FACE OF AN AVUNCULAR OLD GRANDFATHER AND THE HEART OF A MURDEROUS TYRANT.

A TERRIBLE REALITY

Samphan's theory was that, in order to progress, Cambodia must regress; it must turn its back on capitalist exploitation, fat-cat bosses created by the former French colonial overlords, reject corrupted bourgeois values and ideals. Samphan's twisted theory decreed that people must live in the fields and that all the trappings of modern life must be annihilated. If Pol Pot himself had remained an obscure figure, this theory may have remained a coffee bar philosopy rattling around the boulevards and parks of Paris. Instead, it became a terrible reality.

Between 1970 and 1975 the Khmer Rouge – the Red Army led by Pol Pot – became a formidable force in Cambodia, controlling huge tracts of the countryside. On 17 April, 1975, Pol Pot's dream of power became a reality when his armies, marching under the red flag, entered the capital, Phnom Penh. Within hours of the coup, Pol Pot called a special meeting of his new cabinet members and told them the country was now called Kampuchea. He outlined the plans for his brave new world which would begin taking shape within days.

He ordered the evacuation of all cities and towns, a process to be overseen by newly-created regional and zonal chiefs. He ordered the abolition of all markets, the destruction of churches and the persecution of all religious orders. Although privileged himself, in having been educated abroad, he harboured a loathing for the educated classes, and so all teachers, professors and even kindergarten teachers were ordered to be executed. The educated peasant, Pol Pot, feared the educated classes.

The first to die were the senior cabinet members and functionaries of Lon Nol's regime, followed by the officer corps of the old army. All were buried in mass graves. Then came the evacuation of the city, towns and villages. Pol Pot's twisted dream was to put the clock back and make his people the dwellers of an agrarian, Marxist society. Pol Pot was aided by his evil deputy, Ieng Sary. Doctors were murdered because they, too, were 'educated'. All religious groups were exterminated because they were 'reactionary'. The term Pol Pot used for his extermination policy was '*Khchat-khchay os roling*' – it translates as 'scatter them out of sight'. The sinister reality meant the death of thousands.

Below: ***Cambodian defence minister, Keieu Sampen receives a warm hug from Prince Sihanouk (right).***

Buddhist temples were desecrated or turned into whorehouses for the troops or even became abbatoirs. Before the terror, there were some sixty thousand monks in Cambodia; after it was over, just three thousand returned to their shattered shrines and their holy places of worship.

Pol Pot also decreed that ethnic minorities did not, in fact, exist. Vietnamese, Thai and Chinese festivals, languages and cultures were ruled illegal, to be practised under punishment of death. His was to be a pure Khmer society. The deliberate and forceful eradication of ethnic groups fell most heavily on the 'Cham' people. Their ancestors had formed the Kingdom of Champa, once a country in what is now Vietnam. The Cham migrated to Cambodia during the eighteenth century to live as fishermen along Cambodia's rivers and the Tonle Sap lake. They were an Islamic people and were, perhaps, the most distinctive ethnic group in modern Cambodia, for they never adandoned or diluted their language, cuisine, costume, hairstyles, burial customs or religion.

The Cham were obvious targets for the young fanatics of the Khmer Rouge who fell upon them like a plague of locusts. The villages were torched, the people marched into the swampy, mosquito-plagued hinterland, fed pork – strictly against their religion – and the religious leaders executed. When villagers resisted whole communities were murdered, their bodies flung into huge pits and covered over with lime. Of two hundred thousand Cham people alive before the new order, barely one hundred thousand survive today. Those who survived the initial terror found that life

Right: ***Buddhist monks mourn the dead killed by the Khmer Rouge.***

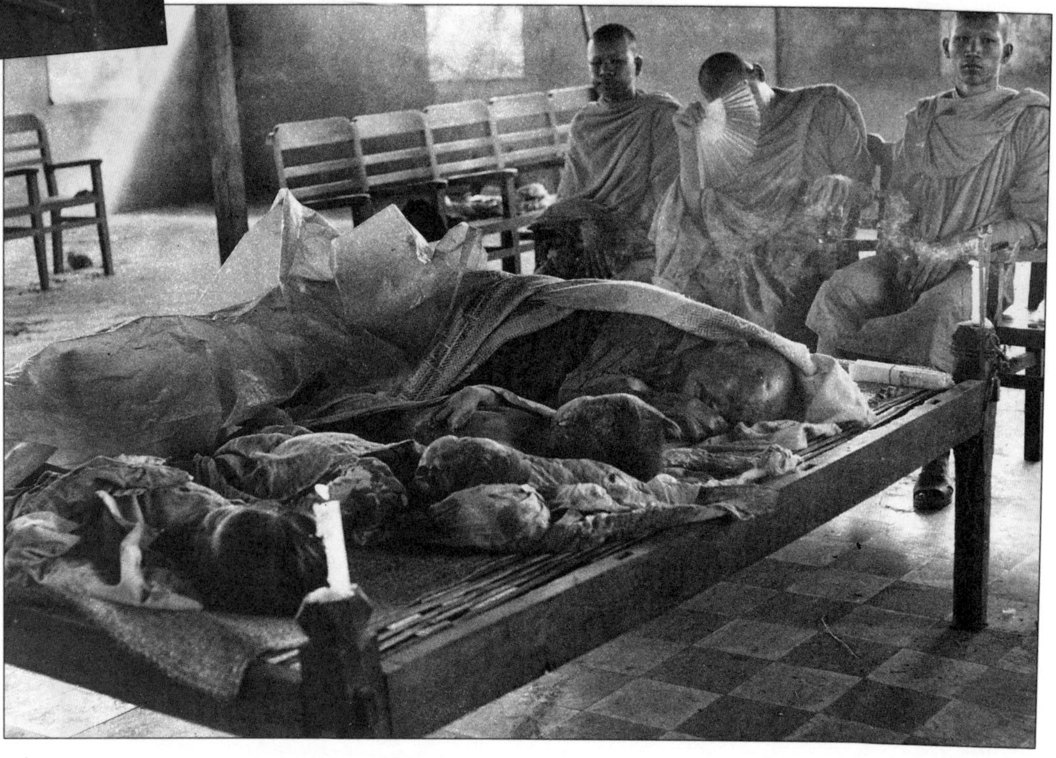

BUDDHIST TEMPLES WERE DESECRATED OR TURNED INTO WHOREHOUSES FOR THE TROOPS.

under the new regime was infinitely harder than a quick death – hence the phrase 'Land of the Living Dead', coined by those forced to live under these conditions.

BOURGEOIS CRIMINALS

Pol Pot believed that all adults were tainted by feudal, bourgeois attitudes, with 'sympathies' for foreign regimes which Pol Pot had decreed were alien to the national way of life. Urbanites, in particular, were rooted out and placed in work camps where hundreds of thousands were literally worked to death or murdered if they spoke French – a major crime in Khmer Rouge eyes because it showed a bourgeois attitude, with a link to, and sympathy with, the colonial reign of the past.

In vast encampments, devoid of any comforts save a straw mat to sleep on and a bowl of rice at the end of every day, the tradesmen, dockers, clerks, bankers – many alive only because they managed to hide their professions – and numerous other citizens, toiled in conditions that would have shamed Japanese prison-of-war camps in the Second World War. The camps were organized, much like the concentration camps of the Nazis, to ensure that 'natural selection' took its toll of the aged and the ill, the very young, and pregnant women. Given a poor diet, deprived of strength, hundreds and thousands succumbed to disease, starvation and the clubbings of their brutal overseers. With no medical men to treat them, save for the attention of a few 'traditional' herbalists whom the new government tolerated, the life span of a prisoner in the camps was pathetically low. They were frog-marched out at dawn into malaria-ridden swamps where they worked twelve hours a day, planting rice and clearing jungles in futile attempts to reclaim more farmland. Then they were frog-marched back at night, under gunpoint and often under the blows and bayonet-thrusts of their guards, to a bowl of rice, gruel and a morsel of dried fish. Then, exhausted though they were, they had to endure Marxist indoctrination sessions, when irredeemable bourgeois elements were rooted out to be taken away for punishment while the others chanted, parrot-fashion, the benefits and joys of the new state. There was one day off in every ten, when people could look forward to twelve hours of indoctrination. Wives were separated from

Above: ***A weary soldier is welcomed by hysterical refugees fleeing the guerilla onslaught.***

THEY WERE FROG-MARCHED OUT AT DAWN INTO MALARIA-RIDDEN SWAMPS WHERE THEY WORKED TWELVE HOURS A DAY

To re-inforce his battle against enemies real and imagined, Pol Pot set up a system of interrogations, tortures and executions in his prison camps. Much like the Spanish Inquisition of old, Pol Pot and his henchmen knew that all who came through the portals of these grim places were guilty – all they had to do was to confess that guilt. To convince its followers that cruelty was necessary and good for the nation, the regime taught its young bureacrats that torture had a special, political significance.

Taught by the Chinese, the Khmer security officers were enmeshed in a hard and cruel ideology, revealed in documents captured after the overthrow of Pol Pot. These dossiers show that torture attained a high level in his nation. One document, the 'S-21 Interrogator's Manual', later handed over to United Nations' investigators, reads: 'The purpose of doing torture is to get their responses. It's not something we do for the fun of it. Thus, we must make them hurt so they will respond quickly. Another purpose is to break them psychologically and make them lose their will. It's not something that is done out of individual anger or for self-satisfaction. Thus we beat them to make them afraid but absolutely not to kill them. When torturing them it is necessary to examine their state of health first and necessary to examine the whip. Don't greedily want to kill them. Politics is very important whereas torture is secondary. Thus the question of doing politics takes the lead at all times. Even when

their husbands, their children were either put to work at the age of seven or given away to the barren wives of party functionaries, so as to be brought up in the mould of fanatical warriors of the revolution. Pol Pot was a thorough man.

Bonfires were made of the books from universities and schools, as wretched, maltreated citizens were forced to chant as the works of civilisation perished in the flames. There were 'hate-ins', when people were whipped before pictures of members of the old regime. It was a nightmare world, sinister and hopeless, for the Cambodian people were literally isolated from the world. There was no postal service, no diplomatic ties with any country, no telephones and no travel; it was truly a nation lost to the world.

questioning it is always necessary to do constant propaganda.

TORTURE WITHOUT REASON

'At the same time it is necessary to avoid any question of hesitancy or half-heartedness, of not daring to do torture, which makes it impossible to get answers to our questions from our enemies, which slows down and delays our work. In sum, whether doing propaganda or torturing or bringing up questions to ask them or accusing them of something, it is necessary to hold steadfastly to a stance of not being half-hearted or hesitant. We must be absolute. Only thus can we work to good effect. We torture them but forget to give the reason first. Only then do they become totally helpless.' The notorious Chinese water torture, crucifictions and suffocations with a plastic bag were three among numerous torture methods practiced by the evil men of the Khmer Rouge.

The S21 facility, from which the document took its name, was the most infamous institution in the whole of Cambodia. Based in the north-east of the country, at least thirty thousand victims of the regime died there. Only seven prisoners are known to have survived – prisoners kept alive because they had administrative skills necessary to their overlords in the running of the dreadful place.

Torture was only one instrument of fear brandished over the heads of the cowed populace. The frequency with which people were executed was another. Many times, inmates in the new country camps were caught eating the flesh of their dead comrades in their desperation for food. The penalty for this was a horrible death of being buried up to the neck in mud and left to starve and thirst while ants and other creatures gnawed at the victim. Then the heads were cut off and stuck on pikes around the settlement with the words painted on a sign hanging from the neck: 'I am a traitor of the revolution!'

Dith Pran, a Cambodian interpreter for American journalist, Sydney Schanberg, emerged from the years of slaughter as a witness to the horrors of Pol Pot's reign. His own experiences, including his threatened execution, were chronicled in the film 'The Killing Fields', in which the torment of the Cambodian people was, for the first time, starkly revealed to the world. Pran's journey from his civilised childhood to a prison camp, where he pretended to be illiterate in order to survive, was a harrowing tale that reduced audiences to tears of pity. 'Many times,' said Pran, 'I prayed that I was dead rather than having to endure the life that I was forced to live. But some of my family had gotten away to America and it was for them that I carried on living. It was a nightmare time.'

Below: ***A Khmer Rouge soldier menaces civilians with his gun. The population of Phnom Penh were quickly subdued by the thugs of Pol Pot's army.***

STACKS OF SKULLS

Pran was one of the lucky ones who survived the Asian holocaust to be reunited with his family in 1979 in San Francisco. Even now, the mass graves of the unknown, unnamed dead continue to be unearthed in remote corners of the sad country, the skulls stacked against the graves like so many footballs.

It was military muscle and not moral right that, in the end, halted the bloodbath and allowed for some semblance of sanity to return to the blighted land. Britain had, it must be acknowledged, spoken out in 1978 against alleged human rights abuses, after receiving reports, through intermediaries in Thailand, about the reign of terror in Cambodia, but the protest was ignored.

Opposite, top: ***Peasants feared that they would be forced to join the 'intellectuals' in the labour camps.***

Opposite, bellow: ***Coils of barbed wire marked the Cambodian border with Thailand.***

Above: ***The fall of Phnom Penh is celebrated by young guerillas of the Khmer Rouge.***

Britain reported to the United Nations Commission on Human Rights, but the hysterical Khmer Rouge representative responded: 'The British Imperialists have no right to speak of the rights of man. The world knows well their barbarous and abject nature. Britain's leaders are living in opulence atop a pile of rotting corpses while the proletariat have only the right to be unemployed, to steal and prostitute.' Regrets were sent from Pol Pot flunkies who said that they were too busy to attend UN enquiries on the allegations to the commission hearings in New York.

In December, 1978, Vietnamese forces, who had been skirmishing for years with the Khmer Rouge over a disputed border region, launched a major offensive with mechanised infantry divisions and full armoured support. The infrastructure of Cambodia had disintegrated so badly by this time, that battlefield reports had to be biked great distances to Khmer Rouge command posts because there were no telephones left in operation.

The Vietnamese, early in 1979, found themselves masters of a blighted land. Pol Pot had fled in his white armoured Mercedes from Phnom Penh, just hours before the Vietnamese troops arrived to liberate the ghostly city. He went scurrying back to his masters in China, glad of the sanctuary, but bitter that they had not come to his aid in resisting the well-armed and determined North Vietnamese onslaught.

'US SURVIVORS REMEMBER OUR FAMILIES BEING TAKEN AWAY, MANY OF THEM, AND OUR FRIENDS BRUTALLY MURDERED.'

Massive amounts of aid flooded into Cambodia as the world realized the full horror of the Khmer Rouge regime and the devastation of the country. The Khmer Rouge were, like the Nazis, particularly methodical when it came to detailing their crimes; investigators found daily logs of shootings, torture, hundreds of photo albums of those to be executed – including those of wives and children of 'intellectuals' liquidated in the earliest days of the terror – and the detailed loggings of the infamous killing fields. These fields, intended to be the basis of the worker's Utopia, a land without money or want, became, instead, the burial pits of a people crushed under the yoke of a cruel tyranny.

Pol Pot seemed to fade into the background but has emerged in recent years to become a major political force vying for power in this embitttered region. Like all tyrants, he said that mistakes were made by those under him, that he had faced rebellions on all fronts and that those who died were 'enemies of the state'. In 1981, back in Cambodia, he told a meeting of old friends at a secret location near the Thai border that he was 'too trusting. My policies were sound. Over-zealous regional commanders and sub-district personnel may have mis-interpreted orders. To talk about systematic murder is odious. If we had really killed at that rate, we would have had no one left to fight the Vietnamese. I have been seriously mis-interpreted.'

ANGEL OF DEATH

Misinterpretation on the scale of three million dead – almost twenty-five per cent of the population of the nation – seems too small a word to describe what was done in his name and under his orders. But following Hitler's code, that the bigger the lie, the more people will believe it, Pol Pot has, once again, become a power-player in the region and is able to rally forces in the countryside that continue to believe in him, and are still loyal to him. Now he is a major force once again, only waiting to ride into the country, like some avenging angel of death, to finish off what he started before: his great agrarian revolution.

For Dith Pran and other survivors, the prospect of Pol Pot's return to power, the possibility that he will plunge his tortured land into new depths of depravity, fills them with horror. When the United Nations first announced that the Khmer Rouge would be part of the power-sharing peace process in Cambodia, Pran said: 'I am still shocked when I see the Khmer Rouge flag flying on UN territory. How would you feel if you were Jewish and you saw Hitler's flag flying at the United Nations? Some people went on a fast for three days to protest this, but I did not. I have starved for four years and that is enough for any man.'

There is international lobbying for world governments to have the Cambodian massacres recognized as war crimes in the same way as the Hitlerian genocide of the Jews has been recognised. Yang Sam, of the Cambodian Documentation Commission in New York, is the Cambodian equivalent of Simon Wiesenthal, the Nazi death camp survivor who, from his office in Vienna, devotes his life to tracing and collating evidence against Nazi war criminals. Sam, a survivor of the terror, collects information against the butchers of his own land. He said: 'Those most responsible for the Cambodian genocide – the cabinet members of Pol Pot's regime, the central committee of his Communist party, the Khmer Rouge military commanders whose troops committed so much of the killing, those officials who oversaw, directed and ran the nationwide network of torture chambers, prison-execution centres and extermination facilities – continue to remain active in Cambodia and international political life. Based in enclaves along the Thai-Cambodian border, they conduct guerilla war seeking to return to power in Phnom Penh. They have not been held accountable for their crime under international law and that is a tragedy of monumental proportions.

'Us survivors remember our families being taken away, many of them, and our friends brutally murdered. We witnessed members of our families and others die of exhaustion from forced marches and slave labour, and from the brutal conditions of life to which the Cambodian people were subjected by the Khmer Rouge.

'We also saw Pol Pot's soldiers destroy our Buddhist temples, end schooling for our children, suppress our culture and eradicate our ethnic minorities. It is difficult for us to understand why the free and democratic nations of the world do not take action against the guilty. Surely this cries out for justice?' But there is no justice here.

WE WITNESSED MEMBERS OF OUR FAMILIES AND OTHERS DIE OF EXHAUSTION FROM FORCED MARCHES AND SLAVE LABOUR.

Below: ***The legacy of the Pol Pot years. The skulls of the anonymous dead serve to remind the world of the man's dreadful regime.***

LAMMERDING
Butchery at Oradour

The Nazis were infamous for their brutal reprisals against partisan fighters. But the villagers of Oradour did not die for their brave resistance. They were slaughtered to avenge the greed of a few German officers.

The tiny hamlet of Oradour-sur-Glane, a village not too far from Limoges in South-Western France existed for close to one thousand years without any more trouble than a bad harvest or blocked drains. Even the conflagration of World War Two had passed by these simple peasant people. Occasionally, they saw German soldiers passing through, or heard the freight trains in the night taking men and supplies to the front after the Allied invasion at Normandy, but to all intents and purposes, the attack that Adolf Hitler had launched against their countrymen had left them relatively unscathed.

Until, on a hot day in June 1944, the soldiers came.

The troops of the 2nd SS Panzer division *'Das Reich'* entered Oradour and, in an afternoon of frenzied butchery, massacred its inhabitants. The men were taken away to a barn and shot, the women locked in the church which was then set ablaze with hand grenades. Every building was dynamited, every animal killed, every child rounded up and sent off to concentration camps. In the madness of that hot June day over six hundred of the citizens of Oradour died at the hands of the Nazi butchers. The question constantly asked by historians is – why? The common explanation, accepted down the years, has been that the villagers were punished by the SS because of increased French resistance activity in the region, following the success of the Allied landings. But another theory has surfaced which deserves consideration – the theory that the villagers were not, in fact, meant to die. Instead, they were supposed to turn over large quantities of gold that the Germans – mistakenly – believed was hidden in the sleepy hamlet.

Oradour stands today as a ghost town, preserved as it was after the last explosion and last round had been fired on that day, nearly fifty years ago. The burned-out car from which the town doctor was hauled and executed, still lies abandoned on the cobbled streets. In the burned and charred butcher's shop remain his meat scales, in the house opposite is a broken sewing machine – all artifacts testifying to a close-knit community that was literally wiped from the face of the earth.

It was a hot Saturday afternoon, just four days after the Allies had gained their foothold in France with Operation Overlord, that a company from the Das Reich division arrived in Oradour. Many were enjoying the serenity of the day – men fished from the banks of the River Glane, others sipped pastis and played *petanque* at the village café.

The SS men, who rode in on half-tracks, in lorries and on motorcycles, were veterans of the Russian front, men who had fought in the 'war without rules' unleashed by their Führer against Slavic 'inferiors'.

ON THAT HOT JUNE DAY, OVER SIX HUNDRED CITIZENS OF ORADOUR DIED AT THE HANDS OF THE NAZI BUTCHERS.

Above: ***Some of the villagers were lined up against this wall and shot by the SS. Their bodies were then burned.***

Das Reich division were Waffen SS, the fighting SS elite and had conducted their war with ferocity. By all accounts, they did their grim duty in the East, as they were instructed by their Führer, and were responsible for untold massacres of the civilian population.

The division that arrived in Montauban, France, in 1944, was a lot different from the one that went to war against the Soviet Union in Operation Barbarossa. General Heinz Lammerding, its commanding officer, was highly decorated – but he had seen the flower of German youth, in the ranks of his division, fall in their thousands. In March 1944, twelve thousand five hundred of the fifteen thousand men that composed this fighting unit were killed and captured on the Russian front in the actions around Cherkassy. The two thousand five hundred survivors, sent to Montauban to become the nucleus of a new division, found themselves surrounded by men of numerous nationalities who had chosen to fight for the swastika. Not unnaturally, the survivors of the Eastern Front regarded themselves as superior in race, attitude and élan to the many other nations that now constituted Das Reich's ranks.

RETALIATION AGAINST THE FRENCH FOR ACTS OF SABOTAGE WAS SWIFT, BRUTAL AND ARBITRARY.

After the Allied onslaught on Normandy, Das Reich was stirred from its days of rest and relaxation, and ordered to begin the long move northwards to the front. And every inch of the way they were targeted by the *Maquis*, the French resistance. With the liberation of their land in sight, and with Allied air superiority ensuring ample supply drops, the French dogged the German advance northwards. Attacks and sabotage had become so commonplace the Germans were stopping to check every piece of horse manure in their pathway in case it was a bomb, for just such a booby trap had claimed the life of three soldiers.

Above: ***Scene from the post-War trial of twenty-one German soldiers accused of the murders at Oradour.***

Retaliation against the French for acts of sabotage was swift, brutal and arbitrary. German soldiers of Das Reich division took part in these loathsome reprisals against innocent civilians and they followed the Führer's orders demanding harsh punishment for anyone who raised arms against his armies. The raids on villages and towns became known as *ratissages*, and it became standard practice for the SS men to fill their pockets with plundered loot on these killing missions. Indeed, Lammerding and two officers under him – Major Otto Dickmann and Helmut Kampfe – were also not averse to stockpiling some money for after the War. All three, in late night discussions over the General's finest cognac, were convinced that the War was going to end in the total and utter defeat of Hitler. With such an eventuality in sight, the acquisition of a nest-egg seemed the logical thing to do.

Dickmann was based in St Junien, not far from Oradour, and was guardian of a single, special truck in the divisional transportation corps. He said it contained divisional records and the 'order of battle', or make-up of the formations which comprised the unit. He ordered an Austrian Lieutenant, Bruno Walter, to double the guard on this vehicle.

Dickmann was nervous in St Junien on the night of 9 June, not least because he believed that there were no fewer than two thousand armed resistance *marquisards* in the town, waiting for the slightest opportunity to launch an attack against him, his men or his transport.

THE GOLD BOOTY

But there were no divisional records on board the truck, no order of battle plans. It is believed to have contained more than six million pounds worth of gold – at today's prices. This was the booty that would guarantee Dickmann, Lammerding and Kampfe an easy retirement at the end of the war. They could not send it back to Germany for fear it would be bombed, intercepted or stolen. Besides, the railway network was rapidly disintegrating under Allied air assaults. A third factor – their fear of the disapproval of Heinrich Himmler, chief of the SS, should he learn that they had looted on such a scale – convinced them that they were left with no alternative but to carry their spoils with them into the front line.

The Resistance was aware of the presence of Das Reich division and knew that it was soon to be on the move again, in preparation to deploy its three hundred heavy tanks and thousands of men against the Allies on the beaches of Normandy. The British had warned the Resistance that it feared the Germans could be in the fighting zone within three days; the French were asked to harass their progress every inch of the way. Dickmann and his superiors knew this – hence the tension felt by those guarding the 'special' truck.

On 9 June, at midnight, Dickmann ordered the truck and a detachment of armed SS men to take the first leg of a journey to move the gold northwards. One plan the trio had devised was to store it in the Loire valley region, while they went up to the front line for the battle. Whatever happened, Dickmann had to get the gold out of the Resistance-infested area as quickly as possible. The night he chose to

Below: ***Captain Kahn (inset) ordered the massacre. Photographs of victims (main picture) were used as criminal evidence.***

THE YOUNG AND RECKLESS RESISTANCE MEN, SEEKING VENGEANCE FOR YEARS OF NAZI OPPRESSION, LAUNCHED AN ILL-PREPARED AMBUSH.

Right: ***Robert Hebras was one of the few survivors, but he was wounded in the attack.***

Below: ***The sad remains of the villagers were mute testament to the Nazi atrocity.***

move was one of chaos and madness for the Germans. Although reprisals were still gruesome and swift, the authority of the Nazi occupiers was rapidly breaking down, as the French sensed that their own liberation was close; they realized that the Allied invasion in Normandy was more than a mere feint or a commando raid, and that the Germans' days were finally numbered. Ambushes, stolen petrol supplies, sabotage – the convoys rolling off that night were plagued by Resistance activity. Dickmann was informed, by his intelligence operatives, that a large group of partisans was operating under the cover of the Forêt de Brigueuil – a densely-wooded area outside of St Junien that covered the road to Bellac, the first stop en route that night for the division. He ordered that the special truck take a different route, one that passed near Oradour. It was a route that was to lead to disaster.

A staff car rolled ahead of the truck, and, in front of that, was a squad of heavily armed soldiers in an armoured half-track. According to plan, they would be in Bellac within thirty minutes, but the local Resistance was to mess up that timing. Planning an ambush on another unit fifteen miles away, the *maquisards* were stunned when they saw the headlights of the half-track glinting at the spot where they had hidden their weapons.

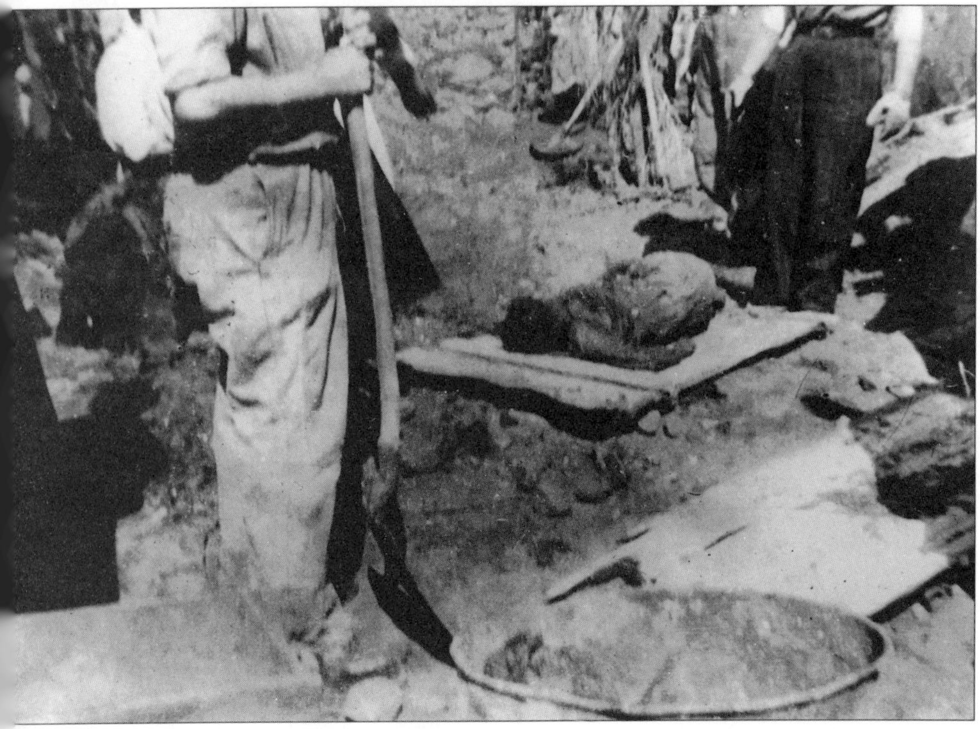

Instantly, plans for the scheduled attack were shelved and the Boche heading towards them became the primary target. The young and reckless Resistance men, seeking vengeance for years of Nazi oppression, launched an ill-prepared ambush. Grenades were hurled at the half-track, killing all of the German soldiers aboard, save one, who scrambled to safety down the road, his clothes smoking from the grenade explosions, but otherwise unharmed. The Germans who survived the grenades were cut down by a withering hail of Sten-gun fire levelled at them from the six partisans under the command of a *maquisard* known only as Raoul.

But the enthusiasm of the attackers far outweighed their military skill. Explosions from the half-track, followed by the car and

truck, spewed shrapnel and burning debris everywhere. That, and return fire, accounted for five of Raoul's men. When the shooting was over and the smoke had cleared, he was the only Frenchman left alive to witness the aftermath, illuminated as it was by the burning wrecks of the staff car and the half-track. The truck had not caught fire. Raoul feared that it might be full of wounded Germans, so he lobbed one more 'Gammon' grenade into the vehicle. When there was no sound from within, he pushed aside the charred and smoking

Above: ***Appalled visitors from other villages came to stare at the devastation.***

tarpaulin, expecting to be confronted with a pile of German corpses. Instead there were wooden boxes, each about the size of a shoe box and each tied down with leather straps. Placing his Sten gun to one side, he used a commando knife to slit the securing straps and open up one of the boxes. It contained gold. Raoul had stumbled on to half a ton of gold.

Risking everything, he hastily removed the gold and dug a shallow trench at the roadside near to the bodies of his dead comrades. One by one, he lowered the thirty-odd boxes into the hole, then covered them with earth. Knowing that if his dead comrades were identified, their families would be murdered by the SS, he poured petrol over each corpse, then over the wreckage in the road, before setting it all ablaze. Then Raoul leapt on his bicycle to ride away from the scene.

When General Otto Lammerding learnt that his *ratissage* loot had been stolen, from under his nose, by the French peasantry he fell into a terrible rage. The half-ton of gold that he intended to use as an escape from the madness of war, to start a new and decent life, had fallen into the hands of the French partisans. He was ordering patrols to rake the countryside for his stolen loot, when he recived the second bad news of the day: Major Kampfe, his compatriot in crime, was reported missing and was presumed to have been captured by the Resistance. Kampfe was a close personal friend and his disappearance fuelled Lammerding's rage to new heights.

RAOUL HAD STUMBLED ON TO HALF A TON OF GOLD.

LOST PENSION FUND

He used Kampfe's disappearance and the attack on the gold convoy – divisional records to anyone who asked – to delay his progress to the front. He did not want to go blundering into a battle while his pension money was in the hands of these filthy peasants. Lammerding requested his superiors let him deal with the perpetrators of the attack on his convoy, and his wish was granted. He consulted Dickmann in a stormy meeting – attested to after the War by an SS telephonist who heard the row – in which he rebuked him for his decision to send the gold with so few soldiers protecting it, yet requested Dickmann's advice on ways of recovering it.

The Germans suspected that the men who had attacked the convoy the previous night came from the town of Oradour-sur-Glane. Not only was it the hamlet nearest the ambush site, but because an SS man who had been captured by the partisans, then managed to escape them, told Dickmann he was 'certain' that Oradour was one of the places where he had been taken as a prisoner.

KILLING FOR LOOT

A notorious Nazi called Captain Kahn, who had distinguished himself by his unspeakable brutality in campaigns against partisans and civilians on the Russian front, was chosen to head the *ratissage* against the inhabitants of Oradour. But historians now believe that his troops were not bent on murder when they entered the hamlet – they believe the Germans simply wished to recover the stolen gold. However, when the peasants denied all knowledge of gold, the mindless brutality favoured by Captain Kahn was allowed to find expression in the soldiers' actions. Dickmann and

Below: ***A monument was erected in Oradour to honour the people whose lives had been so brutally taken from them.***

Right: ***The Nazis were cruel in their reprisals against the French Resistance, but their actions, such as putting a fifteen-year-old boy before a firing squad, only strengthened the French in their guerilla war against the invaders.***

Lammerding may have wanted to kill the entire village, but he would have preferred to trace his stolen loot.

Kahn's vengeance on the inhabitants of Oradour was as senseless, and as vicious as any massacre committed by German troops on the eastern front. He and his soldiers entered the town when it was crowded with people. Farmworkers, who had been toiling in the fields all morning, had returned for lunch when the first half-tracks clattered up the cobbled street, following the line of the railway that connected this village with others in the area. Citizens were rounded up into the church and barn, while a squad of soldiers, with fixed bayonets, moved through fields and outbuildings, chasing out villagers who had sought refuge there. One soldier, Heinz Barth, had actually been born a Frenchman, but had chosen the uniform of the SS. Now, he brandished a machine pistol as he told terrified villagers: 'You'll see the blood flow today!'

The people of Oradour watched and listened as the two hundred and fifty-four buildings, that made up their village, were destroyed by grenades and satchel charges of plastic explosive. Roger Godfrin, a fifteen-year-old boy, ran for his life. 'I told my two elder sisters to run and hide with me,' he explained later, 'but they refused. I somehow knew what the Boche were going to do to us that day.'

MASSACRE IN CHURCH

A white flare, fired high into the sky, was a signal to Kahn that all the villagers had been rounded up. The killing began. The old and infirm, who had been unable to march to the church, were shot where they lay in their little houses. Anyone who bolted for freedom was cut down by machine guns, positioned to cover the streets and fields leading away from the central village square.

When more than four hundred and fifty women and children were packed into the church, the Germans set off a huge charge of explosives, releasing billowing clouds of black smoke to asphyxiate the victims in the church. Then, the soldiers hurled hand

Above: ***Roger Godfrin, the only child to escape the massacre, gives testimony at the military court trial held after the War.***

HE BRANDISHED A MACHINE PISTOL AS HE TOLD TERRIFIED VILLAGERS: 'YOU'LL SEE THE BLOOD FLOW TODAY!'

grenades through the windows; they opened the doors before raking the nave with machine-gun fire. The wooden pews and artifacts caught fire, and the flames consumed most of those trapped in the church, although falling masonry accounted for a number of deaths. Over two hundred men were locked in the barn where they were executed by gunfire. Dickmann, accompanied by two representatives of the hated *Miliciens*, the local militia allied to the Germans, began to question those who had escaped death, demanding they tell him where the gold was hidden. Whenever he met with a denial or ignorance, he shot the person.

In another barn, which had served as execution house to more village men, Jean Darthout was alive, wounded by bullets in his legs. He and three others got away, as did a woman who jumped from a window high above the church altar, although she received five bullet wounds. She hid in a vegetable patch where she was found, close to death, the following day.

THE AFTERMATH

Dickmann, beside himself with rage because the killing and burning had begun before he had had a chance to thoroughly quiz the inhabitants on the whereabouts of the gold, got drunk that afternoon on fine champagne, in the house of a Monsieur Dupic at the farthest end of the village. At seven o'clock that night, as the flames continued to lick at the ruins, Dickmann lurched drunkenly off to his master Lammerding to report that he had failed to find their booty of gold.

Oradour is, today, a ghost town, in ruins, untouched since that dreadful day of destruction. In the little museum that is also a shrine to the dead can be found broken spectacles, love-letters, wine-bottles – the minutae of ordinary peasant life. Many of the victims were burned beyond recognition and are buried in a communal graves in the church and the barns where they were killed. Six hundred and forty-two people died for a hoard of gold about which they knew nothing.

Robin Mackness, a man who once set up the Slumberdown Quilt Company in England, claims he knows what happened to the gold. He wrote a book, 'Oradour – Massacre and Aftermath'. It is a book that many leading historians, including a Second World War French Resistance expert, M.R.D. Foot, believe is the true story of the events in Oradour. It details the story of the lost gold for Mackness was involved, quite by chance,in the story of Oradour long after the War was over.

Above: ***The shattered ruins are called the 'Martryd Village' by the French.***

HE SAID THE HISTORIANS WERE WRONG TO ACCEPT THAT ORADOUR DIED AS A MERE ACT OF REVENGE.

Mackness met Raoul, the French partisan who had buried the gold before fleeing on his bike. In cohorts with business associates in Switzerland, Mackness was smuggling 'black' (illegal) gold across the border from France into Switzerland when he was introduced to Raoul in 1982. The Frenchman told his story, describing the ambush and the reasons why the Germans had selected Oradour as the guilty town. He said the historians were wrong to accept that Oradour died as a mere act of revenge.

Raoul also claimed that he had returned to dig up the hidden gold – stamped with the Nazi *Reichsbank* motif – and that he used some of it to start a business. Now, he wanted to move the remaining loot into a no-questions-asked vault in Switzerland. Mackness says he agreed to help the man, but the mission failed when Mackness was caught by French customs officers. They found twenty thousand pounds worth of the cargo in his car near Lyons in 1982 and he was jailed for twenty-one months.

A SECRET STORY

On his release, Mackness spent years researching Raoul's story and came to the conclusion: 'I don't know exactly what General Lammerding and Major Dickmann said to each other at that meeting on Saturday, 10 June, 1944, but I can guess with some accuracy, because of the story Raoul told me. During my twenty-one months in prison I came to realise that if Raoul's story were true, and there was nothing to finally persuade me that it wasn't, then he and I were probably the only ones alive who knew the secret story behind the events of that day.

'During Dickmann's meeting with his general, he would have learned that Lammerding knew about the ambush from the soldier who had got away. In the event of anything happening to the special unit, it was probable that survivors were given strict orders to report only to those officers most directly concerned – Majors Dickmann and Kampfe or General Lammerding.'

The principal players in the drama are dead and they never told their story while they lived. But it seems certain now, in the light of Mackness' experiences, that the people of Oradour-sur-Glane were killed for their innocence, because they were ignorant of the loot and could not lead a few greedy men to a stolen pile of gold.

HE AND I WERE PROBABLY THE ONLY ONES ALIVE WHO KNEW THE SECRET STORY BEHIND THE EVENTS OF THAT DAY.

Below: ***A wooden cross marks a grave in the churchyard at Oradour.***

WILLIAM CALLEY
The My Lai Massacre

The US army sent untrained rookies to battle in foreign jungles. In some of these soldiers, fear turned to madness and, one dreadful day, the boys of Charlie Company became bloodthirsty barbarians in the village of My Lai.

America went to war in Vietnam in an ideological struggle, a clash between the systems of the West and those of Communism. Young American men marched on to die by the thousand in steamy jungles and snake-infested forests, their blood spilled in unprounounceable places by men with unpronounceable names. But theirs, so said their commanders at the front and the pencil pushers back home, was an honourable cause, fought honourably by the heirs of Patton, MacArthur and Eisenhower. They did not stoop to constructing booby traps of bamboo stakes, smeared with excrement, to cause wounds that immediately became infected, nor did they torture POWs, reducing them to automatons pleading guilt to their 'war crimes' as was the fate of so many Americans captured by the enemy. But any claim to unblemished American morality in Vietnam was cancelled on 16 March, 1968, in a tiny village called My Lai, situated in the Quang Ngai province, on the eastern side of the country where Vietnam bordered on the South China Sea.

On that day, the battle-hardened veterans of Charlie Company, of the American Division's 11th Light Infantry Brigade, entered the undefended coastal plain hamlet and murdered, in cold blood, some five hundred villagers – men, women and babies. In alternating bouts of heated frenzy and cool detachment, the troops of Charlie Company butchered the helpless Vietnamese civilians in an orgy of killing that matched the barbarous acts of the SS in Russia or Poland during the Second World War. Old men were thrown into ditches and bayoneted; pregnant women disembowelled; babies seen crawling away in a paddy field were tossed back on to the heap of corpses from which they had escaped, and were either shot or bayoneted.

The collective madness that engulfed Charlie Company has never been fully understood. Only one man, Lt William Calley, was ever punished for the crime – if three days in a prison can be called punishment. He was released after a presidential review of his case. Over and over again, the men who carried out the massacre, the headquarters' staff in the rear and the American people back home have debated those lethal hours of bloodletting. More than any other episode in that tragic war, My Lai became the symbol of madness, a place that revealed how the strain of war can change decent, respectful, worthy young men into blood-stained barbarians. In the elephant grass and paddy fields around My Lai, the American ideals of truth and justice were cruelly forgotten.

The people of Vietnam were peasant farmers caught up in an horrendous technological war. Napalm, phospherous bombs, Agent Orange defoliant – they had seen the

MY LAI BECAME THE SYMBOL OF MADNESS, A PLACE THAT REVEALED HOW THE STRAIN OF WAR CAN CHANGE DECENT, RESPECTFUL, WORTHY YOUNG MEN INTO BLOOD-STAINED BARBARIANS.

Opposite: ***William Calley Jnr was to play a ghastly role in his country's war against Vietnam.***

Below: ***Captain Medina with his lawyer, Lee Bailey, during a court recess.***

Yankees bring these terrible weapons to the placid villages and many were puzzled by the war. What had they done to incur such wrath from the foreigners?

But My Lai – and every other settlement – in the rural areas of Vietnam were seen by the US commanders as guerilla bases for the 'gooks' – the Viet Cong fighters who, with the support of the peasants, managed to stave off the mightiest nation in the world. Frustration, caused by the difficulties of fighting a hidden, secret peasant army, distilled a certain brutality within the American war leaders; they decided to employ scorched earth tactics, the burning and shelling of villages, as a method of driving the enemy into the open. By the time Charlie Company tramped into My Lai, seventy per cent of the villages in the Quang Ngai area had been razed during the scorched earth policy but anyway, in warfare, mercy is not a ready commodity. 'They were dinks,' said one American infantryman at the time. 'They were gooks, spooks, Charlie. They weren't human beings. We never looked at them as being other human beings. To us they became abstract, things that wanted to kill us, so we killed them first. And that went for the youngest son-of-a-bitch to the oldest. That's what Vietnam did to us.'

A HIGH BODY COUNT

Another soldier, Philip Caputo, a Marine, said that, while orders to kill civilians may not have been written down in black and white, the pressure from the Commanding General in Vietnam, William Westmoreland, on front line units to produce 'kills' was felt heavily by each soldier. Caputo said: 'General Westmoreland's strategy of attrition also had an important effect upon our behaviour. Our mission was not to seize positions or win terrain but simply to kill. Victory was a high body count, defeat a low kill ratio, war a matter of arithmetic. The pressure on unit commanders to produce corpses was intense, and they in turn communicated it to their troops. It is not surprising, therefore, that some men acquired a contempt for human life and a predilection for taking it.'

Charlie Company marched into My Lai with such feelings.

TO US THEY BECAME ABSTRACT, THINGS THAT WANTED TO KILL US, SO WE KILLED THEM FIRST.

Below: ***Captain Medina denied most emphatically that he had ordered a massacre of the people of My Lai.***

The company was initially composed of one hundred and fifty young men who were a typical cross section of the American boys who were sent off to fight in Vietnam. In August 1967, while in their training camp in the USA, they were warned that they may be shipped out to Vietnam at any time. For men like William Laws Calley, now a 2nd Lieutenant with the unit, but who had been a drifter in civilian life, the fun was about to start.

During their training at military installations around America, Charlie Company had gained a reputation as an above-average unit. They excelled in infantry tactics, in jungle warfare simulation exercises and in all-round Army expertise. But there were misgivings among some about the lack of discipline in the squad – and the character of some of the men in it. Michael Bernhardt, one of its number, had trained

force. Their target was a VC battalion that had operated in the region for years, despite massive shelling and the dropping of millions of tons of jungle defoliants intended to lay bare their strongholds. Now technology was abandoned, the human element was sent to quell the guerillas, and it came in the shape of Charlie Company, Alpha Company and Bravo Company.

By the middle of February, a pattern of failure and frustration had established itself among the Americans. Whenever these men fanned out to pre-designated areas, hoping to spring traps on the guerilla positions, they found the enemy had been forewarned and had disappeared. The

as a paratrooper only to find himself teamed up in a unit in Charlie Company. From the moment he joined, he had misgivings about the calibre of his fellow soldiers: 'Some of the men in the company were a little unusual. There were some who were cruel. They weren't the bottom of the barrel – they were men who would have been accepted for military service at any time. I wouldn't expect them to murder or torture anybody...'

BAD OPTIONS

Charlie Company landed in 'Nam', as the troops called it, in the second week of December 1967, and their area of operations was in the Quang Ngai province, a region of innumerable villages where the civilian population had been severely decimated by artillery fire and rapid airborne strikes. The peasants were told to deny their homes to the Viet Cong enemy if they wanted to save their own lives and their land. Sadly, these people were unable to refuse when the Communists chose to use their villages as guerilla bases – the guerillas also threatened loss of life and land. The peasants were trapped between the two opposing sides of the jungle war.

On 26 January, 1968, Charlie Company joined other units to forge a strike force of around five hundred men, destined for search-and-destroy missions in 'Indian Country' – the badlands of Quang Ngai where 'gooks' were said to be operating in

Above: ***William Calley escorted from court after the guilty verdict. He faced a life sentence.***

Top left: ***Attorney Edward MacGill talks to newsmen outside the court.***

bewildered rookies from America were left with nothing but the sounds of their own hearts beating in terror. And in February they began to suffer casualties – a man had half his left side blown away when he stepped on a booby trap. Ron Weber, Lt Calley's radio operator, took a bullet that shattered his kidney when the men of Charlie Company came under a fusillade of sniper fire by a riverbank. He was the first KIA – killed in action – member of the company and it had a profound effect on the men. Calley, leader of the first platoon of Charlie Company, should never have taken his men out into the exposed position that led to Weber's death. This was the first display of his ineptitude as a leader of men.

Daily Mirror

5d. Friday, November 21, 1969 No. 20,499

PINKVILLE

'All of a sudden the GIs just opened fire on the women and children.. I couldn't believe what I was seeing'

THE MASSACRE THAT CHILLED THE WORLD

A HORRIFYING story of a massacre by romping American troops stunned the world yesterday.

Hundreds of Vietnamese peasants were said to have been murdered in cold blood.

And a cameraman, 28-year-old Ronald Haeberle, produced grim pictures of slaughter in the tiny hamlet of My-Lai, which the troops called Pinkville—because the area was coloured pink on war maps.

The photographs show scenes of murder and other atrocities, and of soldiers throwing fuel into a blazing hut with the bodies of villagers lying nearby.

Cowering

One photograph shows women and children cowering in a doorway and holding their stomachs. All of them were killed, Haeberle claimed.

He said yesterday that he was appalled by the brutality.

"I never saw GIs act like that before," he added.

The chilling story came as a bitter blow to President Richard Nixon's bid to win fresh support for his war policies.

Haeberle said the GIs believed that the villagers were Vietcong sympathisers.

As the troops moved in, guns at

From RALPH CHAMPION in New York

the ready, a man holding two small children in his arms walked towards them.

Haeberle said: "They saw us and were pleading. The little girl was saying 'No, no' in English.

"Then, all of a sudden, there was a burst of fire and they were cut down. One machine-gunner did it—he just opened up.

"There was no reaction from the guy doing the shooting. That's the part that really got me—this little girl pleading and they were just cut down."

That was the beginning of the Massacre of Pinkville ... the thirty minutes of killing that left the hamlet destroyed, according to Haeberle.

"A group of people—women, children and babies—were standing around," he said. "The machine-gunner was standing in front of them with his ammo-bearer.

"Then he opened up on all those people in that big circle, and they were trying to run. I don't know how many got out."

There was no mercy for some of those who survived the first hail of bullets, said Haeberle.

GIs went to inspect a pile of bodies. They found one man still alive.

But a soldier "leaned over and finished him off," Haeberle claimed.

He said: "There were two small children, a very young boy and a smaller boy, perhaps four or five years old.

Unarmed

"A guy with an M16 rifle fired at them and the older boy fell over to protect the smaller boy.

"Then they fired six more shots. It was done very businesslike."

Haeberle told of fifteen unarmed Vietnamese who were spotted walking along a dirt road.

"The GIs just opened fire on the women and children," he said.

"Besides that they were shooting at people with grenade-launchers. I couldn't believe what I was seeing."

Then Haeberle told of his horror as troops found a group of mothers and children. He said:

"A GI grabbed one of the girls and started stripping her. They were kneeing the mother away from protecting her daughter—she must have been around

Continued on Back Page

THE SURVIVOR In Vietnam, Do Chuc, 40, who lived through the slaughter, said: "We thought such things were just part of the war."

'North Vietnam cannot defeat or humiliate the United States. Only Americans can do that'

President Nixon in a TV and radio report to the nation on Vietnam policy on November 4.

Above: ***The British newspapers carried banner headings about the dreadful war crime.***

'I THINK I PROBABLY SAW PEOPLE BEING TORTURED TO DEATH.'

Unfortunately it would not be his last and his weakness was to prove disastrous.

Calley, 5ft 4ins in height, who volunteered for army duty just days before he was drafted, was perhaps typical of the men the army got, rather than the men they wanted. By the time he was wearing fatigues, anti-war sentiments in the USA were being openly expressed, as draft dodgers fled to Canada, peace marchers burned the American flag and people spat on returning servicemen home on leave from the war zone. In such a climate, the army needed everyone they could get to keep the billion pound-per-month war going. In such a climate William Laws Calley, failed diner cook, car wash attendant, insurance clerk and railway ticket collector, became, when he was twenty-two years old, an officer in the United States Army. It is a proud office.

Patrols through the steamy jungle and paddy fields continued and Charlie Company continued to take casualties. They also took some prisoners, but now the one-hour lectures they had received on the Geneva Convention regarding the treatment of prisoners-of-war were entirely forgotten. The sharp end of war had already eroded their morals. They now, as a matter of course, indulged in the brutal, casual beating of suspects. Fred Widmer, who later came to be called 'Mr Homicide' for his acts in My Lai, recalled in the book 'Four Hours In My Lai', by Michael Bilton and Kevin Sim how decency was lost to the men in Charlie Company. He said: 'The first time I saw something really bad was the point at which we stopped taking prisoners. A couple of shots and they were done. As time went by, things were done, ears were cut off, mutilations.

TESTING THE ENEMY

'One prisoner had his arms tied straight out on a stick... Lit cigarettes were put inside the elastic of the guy's pants and we watched him dance around because they were burning his ass. I think it was a bit of making him talk and a bit of venting our frustration. I don't remember what happened to them. The more it went on the more you didn't trust anyone. You didn't believe anybody because you didn't know who was who, you didn't know who the enemy was.

'As we went on, more and more prisoners would be executed. I would say it was a regular occurrence. I did abuse someone, a *papa san*, a prisoner. I found myself doing the same things that had been going on all along. We cut the beard off him – this was an insult. A *papa san* with a beard is considered as the wise man, and to cut off their beard was a real sign of disrespect to them. You found yourself punching them around, beating them up, trying to get them to talk. I never tortured anyone to death. I think I probably saw people being tortured to death.' It was a sad admission.

The distinction between peasant soldiers and peasant farmers was lost in this dirty war game. In the imagination of the over-burdened, terror-stricken soldiers of Charlie Company, the Vietnamese people were all 'gooks'. They all had to die.

THE MISSION

Charlie Company, reduced to one hundred and five men because of sickness, death and injuries, were informed on 15 March, that they were scheduled for a search-and-destroy operation on the following day. The village of My Lai, so Calley and his men were told, was the HQ for the elusive 48th Battalion of the VC that Charlie Company had been trying to find ever since their arrival in Vietnam. The men were told that the civilian population would be evacuated by the time the unit arrived at 7.30am. Anyone remaining would be gooks – VC – and they could deal with them in the way enemy soldiers are treated.

No written notes about the briefing of this operation exist. But the people who took part in it say that every man was under no illusions that the drift of the orders was simple: the destruction of all buildings, the slaughter of livestock and the taking of a few prisoners for interrogation. The rest would be consigned to hell. Sergeant Kenneth Hodges remembers his briefing thus; 'This was a time for us to get even. A time for us to settle the score. A time for revenge – when we can get revenge for our fallen comrades. It was clearly explained that there were to be no prisoners. Someone asked if that included the women and the children, and the order was: everyone in the village. They were not sympathetic to the Americans. It was quite clear that no one was to be spared in that village.'

The next day the men, equipped with phosphorus grenades, extra ammunition pouches, mortars and side arms were chopered out on board the green 'Huey' heli-

'THIS WAS A TIME FOR US TO GET EVEN. A TIME FOR US TO SETTLE THE SCORE. A TIME FOR REVENGE.'

Below: ***Ronald Haeberle, left, was a photographer. Michael Bernhardt (right) was a serving soldier. Both were to give crucial evidence at the My Lai trial.***

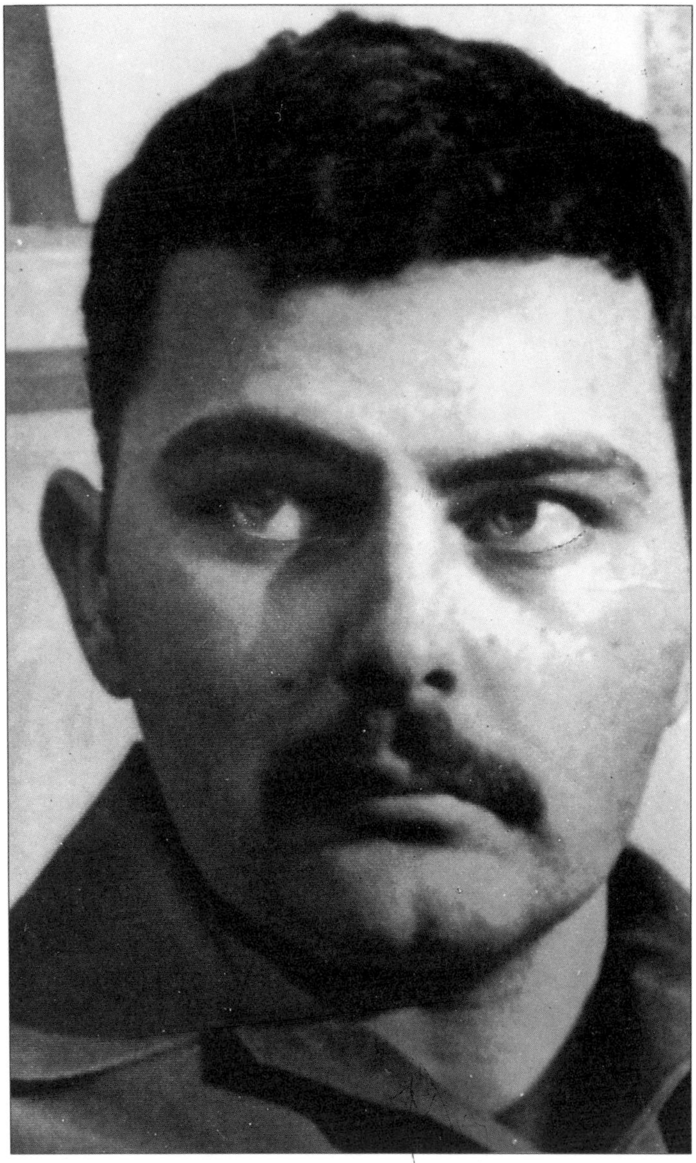

Above: ***Survivors of the massacre claimed that they pretended to be dead so that the soldiers would not attack them any further.***

Right: ***Ronald Lee Ridenhour witnessed the events. He was so shocked that he informed officials in Washington of the atrocity.***

copters for their appointment with death. The countryside of Vietnam appeared beneath them as a patchwork quilt of greens and browns, with the shadow of their own craft creating eerie silhouettes as they moved across the sky. With them, on the helicopters, were two men who would later be instrumental in confirming events in My Lai – a reporter and a photographer from the Army Information Unit.

THE END OF A VILLAGE

The people of My Lai were following their pattern of traditional village life that morning, as the gunships and troopships approached from the sky and a battery of huge 155mm guns trained their sights upon them. Children played with the pigs in the dirt, the women boiled water on open fires, men drifted off to work in the rice fields. At 7.30 the artillerymen opened fire, sending high explosive and white phosphorus shells into the hamlet. The inhabitants rushed for the crude underground shelters they had hewn for themselves.

Minutes later the barrage lifted and the men from Charlie Company approached the village, weapons fully cocked, grenades at the ready. They walked through the paddy fields, moving abreast in lines, and they were shooting. Courts would later be told that women were being cut down by automatic fire before the company had even reached the village.

Once in the village, all sense of American fair play, of decency and humanity, evaporated. The phosphorus grenades were tossed into the straw huts before the villagers were executed at point-blank range with single shots from the men's M.16 rifles. Private Allen Boyce, who, at the subsequent court hearings into the massacre, pleaded the Fifth Amendment on the grounds of self-incrimination, was seen to stab an old man in the chest with a bayonet, then shoot him in the neck. Then he shot another man and threw him down a well. He lobbed a grenade down after him just for good measure.

None of the villagers was armed. From hut to hut Charlie Company moved, grabbing terrified inhabitants by the hair, bellowing 'VC? VC?' at them and then murdering them in cold blood. The shouts

of '*lai dai*' – come here – filled the air as the villagers ran away and were mown down from behind. Groups of between twenty-five and forty people, who had huddled in ditches at the side of the road, were hit by bullets fired from the soldiers' automatic weapons.

At one point, Captain Ernest Medina, one of the brigade commanders overseeing operations that day, radioed Lt. Calley to enquire why his men had slowed up in their progress through the village. Calley replied that they had encountered a large group of civilians, some sixty in all. 'Take care of them,' came the reply from Medina. There was no question of asking for clarification of orders; Calley lined them up and from a distance of ten feet shot them dead with a machine gun, aided by two subordinates. Then he grabbed the dead women who had dived on their babies in a frantic gesture at saving their lives, rolled them off and shot the children. Women who made a break for the tree line in the distance were shot at with grenades and machine guns. One man fell when a grenade fired from a rifle penetrated his stomach but did not explode. He was shot through the head moments later.

Another fifty Vietnamese were found in a separate ditch at the far end of the village. Crouching low in the fetid water were old men, old women, young women and babies. Calley screamed at his men to put their M.16s on to full automatic and join him in the execution. Magazine after magazine was pumped into the screaming, writhing mass of humanity. The water in the ditch turned crimson with blood.

Animals fared no better. Pigs and cows were mutilated with bayonets, chickens beheaded. The keening of these animals stayed in some troopers' minds more than the screams of the massacred civilians.

MEN GONE BERSERK

On and on roamed the berserk killing machine that was Charlie Company. Children were despatched with clinical detachment. Widmer, Mr Homicide, killed a boy. 'When I shot him, I was sick to my stomach,' he said. 'Soon as I did it I realised: "My God, what have I done?" ' But there were worse, more heinous acts of depravity than Widmer's. Women were raped and mutilated, corpses beheaded, some scalped. None of this stomach-churning slaughter affected the appetites of the killers – by mid-morning they had ceased firing and took a lunch break. But the killing was by no means over.

Prisoners who had been taken to a ravine for interrogation were blown away by rifles fired in their mouths. Another hundred civilians were killed in various actions around the village before the company bivouacked for a night when the soft sounds of the jungle were interrupted by the wails of those people who had not been finished off by the death squads. The flames from the burning remains of the villagers' homes lit the night sky.

Dawn revealed the ghastly reality of the previous day's action. Village men who had been working in the fields returned to find their entire families butchered. Weeping, they buried the dead in mass graves, mothers next to fathers, brothers next to sisters, aunts, uncles, cousins. Not one of

Above: ***Chief Warrant Officer Hugh Thompson used his helicopter to evacuate wounded women and children from the scene at My Lai.***

'SOON AS I DID IT I REALISED: "MY GOD, WHAT HAVE I DONE?" '

these victims had fired a shot in retaliation at these soldiers from a foreign army.

Only one American had been killed by the preparatory artillery barrage.

My Lai had been a victory only for the dark side of war and in the cold light of that day, the US Army began to realise that it had lost forever in Vietnam its status of liberator and defender of freedom. Rumours of a massacre circulated with the speed of a disease among the ranks and soon the brass were being asked awkward questions by the Pentagon. It was only a matter of time before the American nation would know what took place.

Frank Barker, the commanding officer of the task force which mounted the assault on My Lai, and from whom many participants in the massacre say they received their orders to kill civlians, was never able to defend himself – he died three months later in a helicopter crash just as the furore surrounding the slaughter rose to fever pitch. The first the public knew of the mission he led came when a former soldier who was there, and who claimed he had not taken part in the killings, wrote letters describing the My Lai massacre to prominent politicians and government officials in Washington.

WHO GAVE THE ORDERS?

First army, then administration officials began to piece together what had occurred in My Lai. They were given photographs taken by Ron Haeberle, the cameraman included in the mission, who snapped many appalling scenes of the dead. He said, in his statement, that he thought the order to kill women and children must have come from higher up: 'Soldiers just do not start killing civilians in the mass they were doing. This was the first time I have seen something like this. I heard later that the General of the Americal Division praised the task force for the operation, but I take it that he was not told that most of the people killed were unarmed women and children.' His testimony was important.

Stanley Resor, Secretary of State for the army, refused at first to believe the massacre story and the US government assumed that a strategic error had been made, insisting that any civilians who died in My Lai were caught in the cross-fire of a fierce gun battle between Americans and VC troops. However, when Resor received a confidential memo from his staff saying that all indications were of a massacre, he could no longer cover up. Investigators travelled all over Vietnam, South-East Asia and America interviewing the members of the disbanded Charlie Company. They testified with some honesty to their participation in the events of that day.

On 5 June, Calley was recalled to the USA and identified as the man who had thrown the baby back into the ditch. He was formally served notice that he was a

Below: ***William Calley saluted in proper officer tradition after his trial ended in Fort Benning, Georgia.***

★★★ FINAL

DAILY NEWS 10¢

NEW YORK'S PICTURE NEWSPAPER ®

Vol. 52. No. 240 Copr. 1971 New York News Inc. New York, N.Y. 10017, Thursday, April 1, 1971★ WEATHER: Partly cloudy and cool.

CALLEY GETS LIFE TERM

UPI Telephoto

Lt. William L. Calley Jr. salutes as he leaves courthouse at Fort Benning after sentencing.—Stories on page 3 potential suspect in the mass murder enquiry. As it turned out, he became the scapegoat for *all* the men who murdered innocent people that day.

Several officers above him were charged with dereliction of duty and other soldiers charged with murder as the investigation-rumbled on. Five were eventually court-martialled, but only Lt Calley was convicted. There was no contrition from him in the dock; he spoke of his duty to kill the Communists, and how he had been a good soldier. It was, perhaps, this refusal to admit that his acts qualified as war crimes that made Calley the symbolic representative of every man who, that day in My Lai, fired a round at an innocent human being.

While some American citizens sported 'Free Calley' stickers on their car bumpers, and anti-war protestors blamed the generals, and not individuals, for what happened, Calley was eventually Found Guilty of a 'speciman' twenty-two murders on 29 March, 1971 and sentenced to hard labour for life. Less than three days later, he was released from prison on the specific instructions of President Nixon and was allowed appeal. He never went back behind bars again, but spent the next three years under house arrest at his spacious apartment in Fort Benning, Georgia, surrounded by the comforts of home, his tropical fish, his dog and other assorted pets.

On 9 November, 1974 he was paroled a free man but was still a victim of war.

The war is long over, the names of the fifty-three thousand Americans who died there etched into the polished granite war memorial in Washington. For Calley, and for the others who were there that day, it is a war that is never over.

NIGHTMARE OF GUILT

Varnado Simpson is typical of the men who went into My Lai that day. Now forty-four, he has attempted suicide three times, seen his son die from a stray bullet – an act that, he believes, was from God as punishment for the massacre – and he gets through each day with endless bottles of pills. 'Yes, I killed. I cut people's ears off. I scalped. Cutting their throats, scalping. Yes, I did that. About twenty-five in all, I guess.

'I have nightmares, I constantly have nightmares of the children. I can go somewhere and see a face that reminds me of the people that I killed. How can you forgive? I can never forgive myself. I don't let anyone get close to me. The loving feeling was killed by My Lai.'

Calley is now a paunched, balding businessman who works at his father-in-law's jewellery store in Columbus, Ohio. He is not on pills, does not need a psychiatrist, has never expressed remorse.

My Lai is never far from his thoughts, but he never, ever speaks of that village. Several years ago he wrote an autobiography in which he attempted justification for the madness that engulfed him and the men under him. He wrote: 'We weren't in My Lai to kill human beings, we were there to kill an ideology that is carried by – I don't know. Pawns. Blobs. Pieces of flesh. And I wasn't in My Lai to destroy intelligent men. I was there to destroy an intangible idea. To destroy Communism. I looked at Communism the way a southerner looks at a negro, supposedly. It's evil. It's bad.'

It is too late for Calley to learn from My Lai but perhaps not too late for mankind.

Above: ***'Take care of them' was the chilling command from Captain Edwin Medina as Calley and his men moved through My Lai.***

HOW CAN YOU FORGIVE? I CAN NEVER FORGIVE MYSELF. I DON'T LET ANYONE GET CLOSE TO ME.

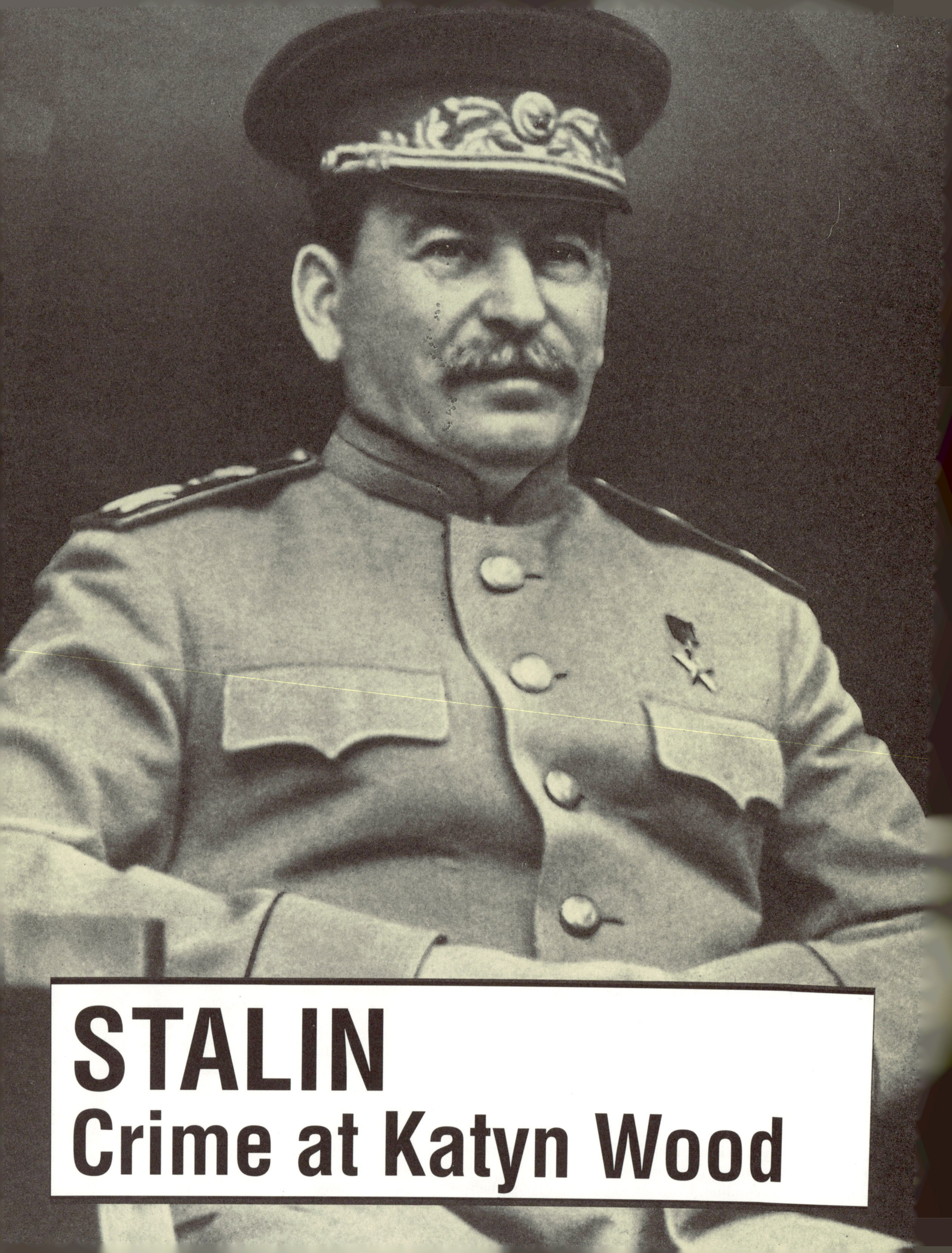

STALIN
Crime at Katyn Wood

In the secret heart of the forest, the proud officers of the Polish army were brutally executed. Even their murderers were so shamed by the killings that they denied the facts. But the dreadful truth of Katyn Wood has not remained hidden.

Adolf Hitler, leader of the German Nazi party, sent his emissary Joachim von Ribbentrop to Moscow in August 1939. He wanted a pact with Josef Stalin, bloodthirsty leader of the Soviet peoples. Yet Stalin represented the Slavic races that Hitler had threatened time and time again, in his manic outpourings, to destroy for ever. And Hitler, in Stalin's eyes, was a fascist running dog who persecuted without mercy the Communists. The former champagne salesman, von Ribbentrop, emerged after several days of diplomatic niceties with his Soviet counterpart, foreign minister Vyacheslav Molotov, to proclaim to a stunned world that a new non-aggression pact had been signed between the two former adversaries. This was *Realpolitik* at its most cynical – the conclusion of distasteful business for the mutual benefit of mutual enemies.

The West viewed the Molotov-Ribbentrop Pact as the precursor to an aggressive war of conquest in Western Europe. With the Soviets promising no action if Germany made 'territorial claims' upon her neighbours, strategists saw that Hitler had effectively silenced his biggest, and a potentially lethal, foe without a shot being fired in anger.

But what the West did not know – and would not find out until a month later, when the armies of Hitler launched their attack on Poland that was to start the Second World War – was that 'the pact' contained a secret clause that divided Poland between Hitler and Stalin. Between them, the two great dictators, who despised each other and the systems each represented, had forged a compact to ensure that this independent nation should cease to exist.

Betwixt the two, Poland became a vassal state. Polish Jews were soon earmarked for destruction by the Nazis, while under the Soviets, the intelligentsia and anti-Communist elements were rooted out for 'special treatment' by the NKVD, the forerunner of the KGB, but that concentrated less on espionage and more on mass murder and political suppression.

Opposite: ***Josef Stalin, the man of steel. He has more blood on his hands than any other man this century.***

Below: ***Polish women weep over their loved ones after the bodies were disinterred.***

Bottom: ***German investigators and Russian peasants exhume the vast mass grave.***

One other segment of Polish national life was hated by both sides – the officer corps of the army who were proud, disciplined, fiercely independent men.

It was precisely because they were troublesome to both dictators, that one of the most heinous crimes in wartime history went unsolved for over forty years. In 1940, four thousand Polish officers, from generals to lieutenants, were bound, shot in the back of the head and buried in massive lime pits, surrounded by thick fir trees that made up the forest of Katyn, near Smolensk in western Russia. All the victims had their hands tied to nooses around their necks which tightened when they struggled; all bore the same single-entry head wound testifying to methodical execution by shooting.

For close on five decades the crime at Katyn Wood was not acknowledged or admitted by the perpetrators. The Germans claimed the Russians did it; the Russians that the Germans were the perpetrators. It was not until the demise of the Soviet Union and the release of KGB files that the truth was out – that the Poles were executed because they were the 'class enemy' of the Soviet people. On 13 April, 1990 Mikhail Gorbachev acknowledged his nation's culpability... forty–seven years after the day that Germany claimed her soldiers in the east had stumbled across the mass graves in the forest.

The events in the clearings of the Katyn Forest during those days of April 1940 make for grim reading. Even now the scars left by the liquidation of these proud warriors remain deep. This is the story of Stalin's massacre of the army allied to Britain – the nation for whom Britain went to war in the first place.

The tale, from being part of the first national army to stand up to Hitler to that degrading execution in the vast mass grave of the Katyn Forest, was a short one for these Polish officers.

Opposite, top: ***Molotov, seated, signs a non-aggression pact with Germany.***

Opposite, below: ***The Russian admission of responsibility for the massacre at Katyn Wood made headlines all over the world.***

Below: ***The villages of Poland were burnt and abandoned as columns of German troops marched through the conquered land.***

IN THESE CAMPS WAS THE BEST OF THE BEST OF POLISH NATIONAL LIFE; EDUCATED, CULTURED, PASSIONATE MEN.

MOLOTOV INFORMED THE POLISH AMBASSADOR: 'THE POLISH STATE CEASES TO EXIST.'

First, Hitler's Stuka dive-bombers and armoured columns brought terror to the civilian population as Operation Case White – the conquest of Poland – began on 1 September. Hitler used a transparently lame excuse for sending his troops across the border; namely, that German soldiers in a frontier post had been killed by marauding Poles. Sixteen days later, with their cities in flames and their armies all but routed, the desperate Poles then had to endure an attack from their eastern neighbour, Russia. Again, it was a flimsy excuse that brought the Red Army pouring over the frontier. In reality, it was the fulfillment of the secret clause in the contemptible Molotov-Ribbentrop Pact.

Stalin camouflaged his military intervention by claiming his soldiers were being sent merely to protect the rights of Byelorussians and Ukrainians, living in Polish territory near the border with the Soviet Union. At 3am on 17 December, hours after Soviet troops, backed up by the death squads of the NKVD, were pouring across the border, Waclaw Grzybowski, the Polish ambassador to Moscow, was summoned to the foreign ministry where he was confronted by Molotov who, shedding all diplomatic niceties, informed him: 'The Polish state ceases to exist. We are aiding you to extricate your people from an unfortunate war in which they have been dragged by unwise leaders and to enable them to live a peaceful life.'

By 5 October, the day the last Polish units ceased fighting, Germany had two-thirds and the Soviet Union one third of Polish territory. Germany took close to six hundred thousand prisoners-of-war; the Red Army captured another two hundred and thirty thousand men. In the wake of the fighting troops came the SS battalions, on the German side, and the NKVD secret police units of Stalin. Both groups were remarkably similar in their initial actions. Round-ups began of intellectuals, university professors, nobles, known radicals, truculent churchmen; anyone who was deemed to pose the smallest threat.

Hitler had used the state as his instrument of repression and murder since he achieved power in 1933, but he was a mere apprentice in the art of massacre compared to Stalin. On his hands was the blood of *tens of millions* of people, murdered across

the vast steppes, shot in the cellars of the NKVD prisons, worked to death in the great Gulag archipelago that stretched over the frozen Siberian wastes. Stalin, in his Kremlin office, decreed that the vanquished Poles in the territory he now ruled would, indeed, receive no treatment that had not already been meted out in large measure to his own suffering masses. None could accuse the Man of Steel of inconsistency in his harshness.

Early in November, after a secret edict from Stalin, NKVD units began separating and moving out from a vast string of POW camps the fifteen thousand Polish officers whom they had captured. They were taken to camps set up in old monasteries that had perished under Bolshevism, all of them within Russian territory. In these camps was the best of the best of Polish national life; educated, cultured, passionate men, many of them reservists who had simply abandoned their comfortable lives to put on a uniform and fight for the land they loved.

Only a handful would ever see it again.

The NKVD were preparing for *mokrara rabota* – the agency's slang for bloodletting. For months the NKVD superiors at the prison camps, that held the Poles, had been sending reports back to their Lubyanka masters, suggesting that some of the Polish officers might be transported to Moscow, where they could be assimilated and indoctrinated into the Soviet system. But Josef Stalin had already made up his mind about their fate.

The liquidations at the Katyn Forest began on 3 April and did not end until 13 May, five weeks later. In the previous week the prisoners were rounded up in their camps at Kozelsk, Starobelsk and Ostashkov and taken in batches to railheads to board cattlewagons for unknown destinations. However, the four thousand four hundred Poles from Kozelsk camp were bound for the forest at Katyn.

HOPE OF REPATRIATION

Since their capture, these men had existed on meagre rations and were given few facilities to communicate with their families. During the days that they were herded into trains, they were given a better diet, kindling hope among them that they were

4 TODAY Saturday April 14 1990 ★★

RUSSIA BLAMES STALIN FOR WIPING OUT 15,000 POLES

50 YEARS ON, KATYN REVEALS THE TERRIBLE SECRET OF ITS 4,254 GRAVES

by OLGA CRAIG

THEY had been told they were going home. Instead, the train taking thousands of Polish prisoners of war across Russia was halted in a remote forest.

The 4,254 officers were ordered out and shot. Their bodies were buried in a mass grave.

The 1941 Katyn massacre was one of the worst outrages of World War Two, but the truth about it stayed an evil secret for 50 years.

It was not until yesterday that the Russians finally admitted Stalin ordered his secret police to slaughter the men and another 10,600 Polish officers whose bodies have never been found.

In an about-turn which stunned the world, Moscow Radio reported the discovery of new archive documents laying the blame firmly at the door of the NKVD, forerunners of the KGB.

Deserted

After the Poles, captured in the Nazi-Soviet partition of their country in 1939, failed to return home, Stalin insisted they had all deserted.

When the mass grave filled with 4,000 bodies was accidently found during forest clearance in 1943, he blamed the horrific mass slaughter on the Nazi invaders.

The Katyn area had changed hands during the war, controlled first by the Russians, then by the Germans.

Letters

But the Russians held the land in April 1940, the day 4,000 officers at Kozelsk camp were told they were being sent home.

They rushed off letters to loved ones saying they were coming back "via Katyn".

When the train jolted to a halt just outside the western town of Smolensk the officers were still in a celebration mood.

Then the doors were wrenched open and they tumbled blinking into the sunshine.

One by one the bewildered men were dragged into a long line overlooking deep newly-dug trenches.

Side by side they stood, trying to make sense of it all.

An order was shouted and a battery of shots was fired. Four thousand Polish officers were shot in the back of the neck by Russian soldiers.

The remains of another 10,600 officers who were held in camps at Starobelsk and Ostashkov have never been found.

Now their families are demanding that the sites of their massacres are revealed too.

They say apologies, compensation and punishment must follow.

The Katyn Family, a Polish organisation for relatives of victims, said it wanted criminal proceedings brought against anyone still' alive who was involved.

The Katyn bodies, stacked in layers, were found by the Nazis in April 1943 and immediately used for propaganda against the Allies.

The Soviets always insisted the officers were killed in 1941 by the Nazis after they invaded the Soviet Union.

Historians

After the war, Poland's Communist governments continued to echo the Soviet explanation.

But most Poles and Western historians had long concluded that the massacre of "class enemies" was committed by the Soviet secret police on Josef Stalin's order in late April 1940.

As Soviet leader Mikhail Gorbachev's glasnost policies took hold, Soviet and Polish historians joined forces to review Katyn and other historical "blank spots".

The Polish side confirmed Soviet responsibility last year, but a promised joint report never appeared.

The Soviets' formal admission of guilt has been timed to coincide with a three-day state visit to Moscow by Polish President Wojciech Jaruzelski.

Radio Moscow's report, based on an official statement by Soviet news agency Tass, made no attempt to play down the outrage.

It said: "The Soviet side expresses its deep regret over the tragedy and deems it one of the most horrifying Stalinist crimes."

Justice

Accepting responsibility for the atrocity has been one of the conditions for improvement in relations between Poland and the Soviet Union.

Solidarity leader Lech Walesa last night called the Soviet admission "an act of moral justice which has been awaited for a long time".

He said: "It's good that criminals admit their crimes."

Foreign Secretary Douglas Hurd said yesterday: "We must remember the heavy weight of history there is in Russia, the terrible things Stalin did, and the terrible things which were done to Russia during the last war.

"Gradually bits and pieces are coming out, a bit gingerly, as the Katyn story shows.

"But it must be right that it should come out and that they should admit the truth."

But the admission has come 50 years too late for some of the surviving families.

"I regret terribly that my mother could not live until this day," said Wanda Zadroza, whose father was murdered in the forest.

She added: "But whatever happens now, it is good that the truth will be finally written in our history books."

HORROR: Gruesome scene when the grave was found in 1943

IN April - May 1940 394 of the 15,000 or so Polish officers kept in the three camps were transferred to the Gryazovetsk camp. The larger part, however, were turned over to the NKVD administrations in the Smolensk, Voroshilovgrad and Kalinin regions and never mentioned in NKVD statistical accounts since.

The discovered archival material puts direct responsibility for the atrocities in the Katyn Forest on Beria, Merkulov and their henchmen. The Soviet side, expressing profound regret over the Katyn tragedy, declares that this tragedy is one of the gravest crimes of Stalinism.

TRUTH: The text of the official statement released in Moscow

Crusade of anguish

A BRITISH officer led the fight for truth.

Sir Frederick Bennett has shared the anguish of widows of the slaughtered Poles. He has seen the letters, now creased and stained with tears, the men wrote to say they were coming home.

Last night the retired major said: "I can't use the word delighted to describe how I feel. Somehow it wouldn't seem appropriate, but you've no idea how relieved I am."

Former MP Sir Frederick, 71, founded the Katyn Association with top Tory Airey Neave, later killed by an IRA car bomb. Sir Frederick had been approached by Poles he befriended as they fought side by side during the war.

"The letters are tragic," he said. "One soldier jubilantly tells his wife he is being sent home by train — via Katyn."

The Russian admission has boosted Sir Frederick's fight for compensation for the 15 Katyn widows still alive in Britain.

Next Saturday he will unveil a plaque honouring the dead at the Katyn monument in Gunnersbury Cemetery, West London. It says bluntly: "Murdered by Soviet secret police under Stalin's orders."

indeed being repatriated to a new life. Each man received three dried herrings, half-a-pound of bread and some sugar. For some lucky few there was even an issue of Russian cigarettes to treasure.

The NKVD wanted the officers lulled into a state of well-being. Had there been any inkling of what lay in store for them,

Above right: ***Red Cross and other officials are shown the grave site by a German officer.***

Above: ***German Red Cross workers search for anything to help identify the corpses.***

Right: ***Jewellery and military insignia found on one Polish corpse.***

there would have been bloody mutinies from the brave prisoners in the camps.

But once at the railheads, away from the camps and their comrades, the treatment changed immediately. New NKVD men were waiting to board them on the trains, men armed with clubs and dogs and with the vicious, four-sided bayonets issued to the NKVD. Many prisoners were severely, gratuitously beaten as they clambered aboard the trains. Waclaw Kruk, a lieutenant, was one of the officers never to return from Katyn.

A diary was later found near his body in which he wrote down his feelings – feelings that must have been those of all the Poles as they moved out of the camps into the unknown. 'Yesterday a convoy of senior

'I AM NOW COMING TO THE CONCLUSION THAT THIS JOURNEY DOES NOT BODE WELL.'

officers left: three generals, twenty to twenty-five colonels and the same number of majors. We were in the best of spirits because of the manner of their departure. Today, my turn came. But at the station we were loaded into prison cars under strict guard. Now we are waiting to depart. Optimistic as I was before, I am now coming to the conclusion that this journey does not bode well.' His diary was found in 1943, near a body tagged 'number 424'.

Another corpse, that of Major Adam Solski, also had a journal near it. Experts who examined it concur that the condemned man wrote the final words less than twenty minutes before he was murdered. It makes sad reading. 'Few minutes before five in the morning: reveille in the prison train. Preparing to get off. We are to go somewhere by car. What next? Five o'clock: ever since dawn the day has run an exceptional course. Departure in prison van with tiny cell-like compartments; horrible. Driven somewhere in the woods, somewhere like a holiday place. Here a detailed search. I was relieved of my watch, which showed 6.30am, asked for my wedding ring. Roubles, belt and pocket knife taken away.'

Journey's end for the soldiers was the Katyn Forest, sloping towards the Dnieper River and not far from the town of Smolensk. Here, gigantic pits had been dug in the sandy soil, within the leafy groves of fir trees and silver birch. Not far from the pits was a building known innocently as The Little Castle of the Dnieper; in reality it was a summer house, a dacha, of the local NKVD and now served as the headquarters of the killing squads who were about to despatch the cream of the Polish army to their deaths.

A SINISTER JOURNEY

The prisoners were taken from the rail cars in what were known as the *chorny voron* – the police buses, which had been a grim feature of Soviet life for years. A glimpse of one of them, in a Soviet street, was enough to send shivers up the back of any innocent observer. These buses were divided into separate steel compartments, each little bigger than a kennel, in which the Polish officers were kept until their turn for execution arrived.

Only one man, a Polish professor, Stanislaw Swianiewicz, saw the killing of his comrades and lived to tell the tale. He was on board one of the trains, but was locked into a compartment by himself, only to be transported to Moscow to face charges of espionage. But he witnessed the scene as his fellow officers were led to their deaths. In the authoritative book 'Katyn' by Allen Paul, the professor was quoted: 'wondered what kind of operation it was. Clearly, my companions were being taken to a place in the vicinity, probably only a few miles away. It was a fine spring day and I wondered why they were not told to march there, as was the usual procedure at camps. The presence of a high-ranking NKVD officer, at what was apparently the simple transferal of several hundred prisoners from one camp to another, could be explained if we were actually going to be handed over to the Germans. But, in such a case, why these extraordinary precautions? Why the fixed bayonets of the escort? I could think of no reasonable explanation. But then, on that brilliant spring day, it never even occurred to me that the operation might entail the execution of my companions.' Such an act was unthinkable.

WHY THESE EXTRAORDINARY PRECAUTIONS? WHY THE FIXED BAYONETS OF THE ESCORT? I COULD THINK OF NO REASONABLE EXPLANATION.

Above: ***A German officer holds up the decomposing jacket of a murdered Polish officer.***

Execution at the pits was to be cold, methodical, production-line work. Machine guns or grenades could not be used; people would run, there would be survivors, there would be an immediate panic among those prisoners awaiting transport from the train to the execution place. Instead the NKVD agents used 7.65mm Walther German-police issue pistols, considered by handgun experts to be the best pistols of their type in the world. NKVD squads would be waiting with fresh guns to replace those that over-heated in the ceaseless slaughter, others with mounds of ammunition.

Once taken, one by one from the buses, the individual prisoners were bound in a particularly gruesome manner – a manner perfected over the years by the murderers from the NKVD. The victim's hands were first tied behind his back, then a second cord was tied over his head at neck level with the victim's greatcoat pulled up over it, like a shroud. From the neck the cord was passed down the prisoner's back, looped around the bound hands and tied again at the neck, forcing the arms painfully upwards towards his shoulder blades. Any attempt to lower his arms put pressure on the neck; repeated pressure would result in strangulation.

AS THE LAST OF THE SAND WAS BULLDOZED OVER THE GRAVES, THE BUTCHERS PLANTED TINY BIRCH SAPLINGS ON TOP.

Below: ***Joachim von Ribbentrop announces details of the cynical pact with the Soviet Union to carve up Poland.***

One by one these brave, noble men were led to the edge of the pits. Many bodies bore the brutal stab-marks of the four-squared NKVD bayonets – proof that, agonizing though their bonds were, they had attempted to struggle for their lives. Each one was despatched with what the Germans called the *Nackenschuss* – a shot through the nape of the neck which caused instant death and limited blood loss. This method had been perfected in countless cellars and execution dens of the NKVD over many years of Stalinist terror.

I SENSED A PROPAGANDA EXERCISE. I HATED THE GERMANS. I DID NOT WANT TO BELIEVE THEM.

They fell into the pits and were stacked like cordwood, one on one, in layers of twelve before lime was sprinkled over them and tons of sand bulldozed back over them. But the tons of sand helped to press the corpses down and literally 'mummify' them as the body fluids and blood was squeezed out. The lime failed to work, so when the advancing Germans discovered the graves of Katyn, the thousands of corpses were well preserved.

On and on went the killing. The NKVD butchers fuelled their spirits with massive quantities of vodka consumed in the nearby dacha. Twelve hours a day for six weeks, nothing but the sound of gunshots echoed from those lonely groves until, finally, four thousand one hundred and forty-three victims were dead. As the last of the sand was bulldozed over the graves, the butchers planted tiny birch saplings on top.

The remaining eleven thousand Polish officers, held in other camps were liquidated at killing sites deeper in Russia. Their graves have never been exhumed but there has since been an admission from the now-defunct Soviet Union that all these Polish officers had been annihilated on Stalin's personal orders.

But Katyn was, and remains, the most significant massacre site. It was a known site, yet for decades it was surrounded by lies and duplicity. It justified a deep-rooted hatred of the Soviet state felt by all the people of Poland.

FRIENDS TURN ON EACH OTHER

It was only a matter of time before those arch-enemies, Hitler and Stalin, were to turn on each other. Hitler had written in *Mein Kampf* that *Lebensraum* – living space – in the east was his single greatest goal. On 22 June, 1941 he set out to achieve that with Operation Barbarossa, the attack on the Soviet Union.

Fifteen hundred miles away from Stalingrad, in the dacha where the NKVD executioners planned the killing of the Polish officers, the soldiers in Lt Col Friedrich Ahrens' signal regiment were having a relatively quiet war.

Ahrens and his men had a strange foreboding about Katyn Wood, the site of the dacha. They heard rumours from the local people about NKVD executions taking place there, and hidden graves. Then, in February 1943, when the German 6th Army was routed at Stalingrad, a wolf unearthed bones in one of the mass grave sites. Ivan Krivozertsev, a local peasant, approached Ahrens and formally informed him of the dark secrets of the forest. NKVD secrecy and planning had not been hidden from the sharp eyes of the peasants.

Below: ***British prisoners-of-war were taken to the site. The Germans wanted to convince the Allies that the massacre was a Russian act.***

The Germans prepared to tell the world of the slaughter of the Polish officers, and Dr Gerhard Buhtz, a professor of forensic medicine from a leading German university, was put in charge of the exhumation and examination of the grave pits, which were opened in early March. For ten weeks the stink of rotten flesh and Egyptian tobacco – the Germans smoked it to mask the smell of the dead – mingled with the scents of moss and pine sap as the murdered men were disinterred and laid out. Some prisoners-of-war, American Lt Col John Van Vliet among them, were taken by the Germans to witness the massacre site. He recalled: 'I sensed a propaganda exercise. I hated the Germans. I did not want to believe them. But after seeing the bodies there, piled up like cordwood, I changed my mind. I told the Allies, after the War, that I thought the Soviets were responsible.'

On 13 April, 1943, at 3.10pm Berlin time, the German radio network officially announced the finding of the graves where the Polish officers had been 'bestially murdered by the Bolsheviks'. The world was stunned into silence, choosing to believe that the report was fabricated by the Nazis. But the Polish government-in-exile, in London, had long harboured suspicions that the Russians had copious amounts of Polish blood on their hands.

On 15 April the Soviets counter-attacked, claiming: 'In launching this monsterous invention the German-Fascist scoundrels did not hesitate at the most unscrupulous and base lies, in their attempts to cover up crimes which, as has now become evident, were perpetrated by themselves. The Hitlerite murders will not escape a just and bloody retribution for their bloody crimes.' Three separate commissions were invited to visit Katyn by the Germans. The first was entirely German, the second composed of scientists and forensic experts from Switzerland, Belgium, Hungary and Bulgaria, and the third was entirely Polish. The evidence was mightily in favour of the German viewpoint. Although the ammunition was

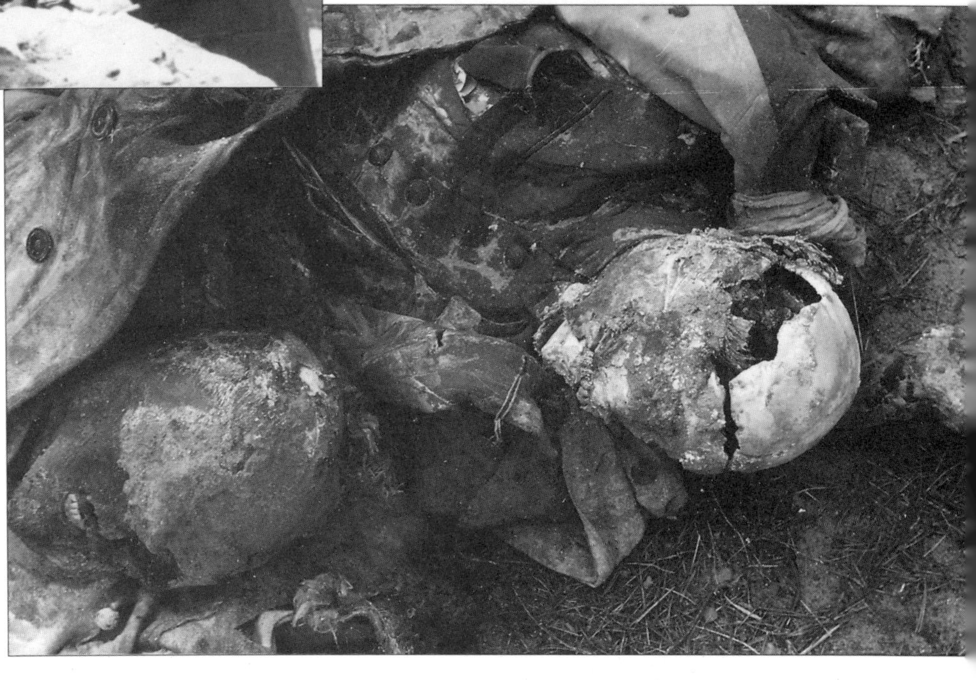

Above: ***Skulls revealed that execution had been carried out with high-calibre weapons used at point-blank range.***

German, records from the manufacturing plants showed it to be batches sold, before the war, to Lithuania only to be siezed later by NKVD police units.

The Soviets claimed that the men were killed by the advancing Germans in 1941 – although not one document with a date later than 6 May, 1940 was ever found on a single corpse. The bayonet thrusts on the bodies were of the four-cornered NKVD type. The fact that there were no insects found in the graves indicated cold weather-burial, not summer as the Soviets claimed – and besides, all the murdered soldiers wore heavy winter clothing.

But their military fight against Hitler had, for the Allied commanders, at that time, a higher priority than a search for justice and truth. Churchill remarked in a cabinet meeting: 'We must not take sides in the Russo-Polish quarrel.' He assured Stalin in a secret communique that he would do his personal best to silence Free Polish newspapers in London over the affair, while he told Wadyslaw Sikorski, the prime minister in exile: 'If they are dead, nothing you can do will bring them back.' President Roosevelt in the White House preferred to believe the Soviet leader's explanation that the murders were committed by the Nazis.

Right: ***A priest prays at the graveside for the Polish officers, who were denied the blessing of the last rites at their death.***

Below: ***Row upon row of corpses, all tied in the same fashion, were pulled from the mass burial pit.***

When the Soviets finally overran the Katyn territory in their great push westwards, they took the opportunity to cover up the massacre of the Polish officers. The ponderously-named 'Special Commission for Ascertaining and Investigating the Circumstances of the Shooting of Polish Officer Prisoners by the German Invaders in the Katyn Forest' went into overdrive to persuade the world that the murders were the work of the Gestapo and *Einsatzgruppen*. The Soviets stuck to their story that the officers had been murdered a year later than was actually the case – and as stories of German atrocities throughout the War began to emerge from all over Europe, there were plenty of people willing to believe the Soviets.

By the time the triumphant Red Army rolled into Berlin in May 1945, the myth that the Germans were responsible for Katyn was firmly planted around the world and in the satellite Eastern European nations over which, in Churchill's words, the Kremlin had drawn an 'Iron Curtain'. In Warsaw, the monument to the dead at Katyn blamed the Nazi invaders; at Katyn itself the inscription read: 'To the victims of Fascism. Polish officers shot by the Nazis in 1941.' The Soviets were operating under the maxim that Hitler once used – tell a lie big enough for long enough and it will metamorphose into truth. They denied any reference to the atrocity if it cast suspicion on their forces. Ewa Solska, the daughter of Major Solski whose diary was found on him, wrote 'killed at Katyn' in the box on her university application form which asked for information about her father. She was expelled for giving this information.

Even at Nuremberg, the great post-war trial for the crimes of Nazism, the Soviets were able to bluff the tribunals that Katyn was a Nazi crime. They could not bluff the Polish people, nor the many people around the world who were slowly caming to realise the enormity of Stalin's crimes.

It wasn't until 1990, at a ceremony inside the Kremlin, that Gorbachev, in keeping with the spirit of his Glasnost reforms, handed President Jaruzelski of Poland a box containing NKVD documents and other files, showing that the officers had indeed been murdered by the NKVD. These revealed that the executioners themselves had been 'liquidated' under Stalin's orders, then buried at an unknown grave site somewhere in Russia. Only four hundred prisoners-of-war from the entire Polish officer corps survived, to be taken to Moscow and other Russian cities, where they proved to be willing Communists. Gorbachev labelled the massacre 'one of the gravest crimes of Stalinism'.

Was it all a big mistake on Stalin's part? Some historians believe that his orders may have been 'misinterpreted' by underlings. Stanislaw Mikolajczyk, the successor to Sikorski in London for the Polish government-in-exile, has his view and claims a Soviet bureaucrat secretly gave him the following interpretation of what happened:

A MISSINTERPERATED ORDER

'Early in 1940 the Red Army sent a staff officer to find what Stalin planned to do with the Polish officers. A planned swap in which the officers would be turned over to the Germans in return for thirty thousand Ukrainians had just fallen through. The Ukrainians were Polish Army conscripts captured by Germany the previous September, and were interned in two camps in eastern Poland. The Germans, at first agreed to the exchange but backed out at the last possible moment, telling the Soviets to take the Ukrainians and keep the Poles. Then came rumours in Moscow that the Ukrainian conscripts and the Polish officers would be organised into special units of the Red Army. Senior commanders were aware of such talk but had nothing specific to go on. The staff officer was sent to get Stalin's clarification. The staff officer saw Stalin and briefly explained the problem. Stalin listened patiently. When the staff officer finished, Stalin supplied him with a written order. Such orders were common, often requested by subordinates as a matter of self-protection. In this case. said the informant, Josef Stalin took a sheet of his personal stationery and wrote only one dreadful word on it: 'Liquidate'.

The staff officer returned the one-word order to his superiors, but they were uncertain what it meant. Did Stalin mean to liquidate the camps or to liquidate the men? He might have meant that the men should be released, sent to other prisons, or to work in the Gulag system. He might also have meant that the men should be shot, or otherwise eliminated. No one knew for sure what the order meant, but no one wanted to risk Stalin's ire by asking him to clarify it. To delay a decision was also risky and could invite retribution. The army took the safe way out and turned the whole matter over to the NKVD. For the NKVD, there was no ambiguity in Stalin's order. It could only mean one thing: that the Poles were to be executed immediately. That is, of course, exactly what happened.'

Many thought Stalin, the Man of Steel would never have had it any other way.

Above: ***The soil in Katyn Wood served to preserve the bodies. This was of considerable help when investigators came to identify bodies and buried papers.***

STALIN TOOK A SHEET OF HIS PERSONAL STATIONERY AND WROTE ONLY ONE WORD ON IT: 'LIQUIDATE'.

ADOLF HITLER
The Holocaust

Germany was humiliated by defeat after the Great War. Despair gripped the nation. But one man promised to return their pride. All they had to do was build gas chambers and kill, kill, kill. So began the most shocking mass murder in the history of the world.

They met at a place called Wannsee, a charming suburb of Berlin with ornate houses and tree-lined streets that looked out over the lake which gave the area its name. It was 20 January, 1942 and the Reich had reached the zenith of its military victories. The swastika flew over the Russian steppes, over the Balkans and Greece, France, the Low Countries, North Africa, Poland, Norway and Denmark. The wars of conquest had ended in total triumph for Hitler's armies so it was now time to put into effect phase two of his doctrine of Nazism. It was time to implement 'The final solution of the Jewish question in Europe'.

No one who followed the rise of Adolf Hitler and his Nazi party was surprised that he had a diabolical plan to eradicate the Jews. Hitler began his campaign of state terror against the Jews soon after he came to power. He passed the infamous Nuremberg Laws which stripped them of property, valuables, human rights and political power. Then he organized the terror, which culminated in the *Kristallnacht* – 'Night of Broken Glass' – in 1938. This involved the destruction of synagogues and Jewish property throughout Germany during a frenzied night of state-sponsored terror. But Hitler wanted 'a final solution to the Jewish problem' and this was to become a euphemism for mass murder.

That is why at Wannsee, in 1942, SS and Gestapo chiefs, led by Reinhard 'Hangman' Heydrich, gathered at a villa, once owned by a Jewish merchant, to plot the logistics for the collection, transportation and extermination of millions of men, women and children who had no place in the new world order. The men in black and grey uniforms drew up blueprints for the greatest state-sponsored murder in history.

Since the Nazi seizure of power Hitler had experimented with mass-killing techniques at euthanasia laboratories where the mentally ill were killed in gas-vans or by lethal injection. When his armies overran Poland and parts of Russia he walled his Jewish enemies up in medieval-style ghettoes where he allowed starvation and disease to kill the people locked within. In Russia his *Einsatzgruppen* – action squad – SS commandos shot hundreds upon thousands of Jews and other 'undesirables'. But

Opposite: ***Adolf Hitler salutes to his followers. Rudolf Hess stands before him.***

Below: ***An SA stormtrooper ensures that shoppers follow the order on the sign: 'Do not buy from Jews'.***

HOESS TOOK A SCIENTIFIC DELIGHT IN SOLVING THE PROBLEMS OF MASS MURDER.

NAMES LIKE TREBLINKA, SOBIBOR, BUCHENWALD, DACHAU AND AUSCHWITZ HAVE NOW BECOME HOUSEHOLD WORDS FOR EVIL.

Right: ***Survivors stand in bitter mourning for their lost families at the memorial erected to the victims of the Holocaust.***

it was not enough. These methods were cumbersome, slow and inefficient. Hitler was determined to bring some Henry Ford principles into the process of mass murder – a production line of death camps that would dispatch the unfortunates at the greatest speed possible.

Herman Goering, Luftwaffe chief whose first task for the Nazis was setting up the dreaded Gestapo, had Heydrich's orders in a letter, written six months before the Wannsee conference. It read: 'I hereby charge you with making all necessary preparation with regard to organizational and financial matters for bringing about a complete solution of the Jewish problem in the German sphere of influence in Europe.'

Heinrich Himmler, head of the SS; Heydrich, head of the SD, the security arm of the same organisation; Adolf Eichmann, and Ernst Kaltenbrunner, Heydrich's successor after his master was assassinated in Prague in May 1942, can be said to be the architects of the final solution. They built the concentration camp network which spanned all conquered Europe.

Names like Treblinka, Sobibor, Buchenwald, Dachau and Auschwitz – Auschwitz, particularly, the most infamous human abbatoir of them all – have now become household words for evil. In these death factories Jews from all over Europe made a one-way trip to hell. And not only Jews – Gypsies, Poles, Slavs, Russian prisoners-of-war, intellectuals, revolutionaries, homosexuals and artists who did not fit into the racial or political mould were despatched. A new breed of men and women, inconceivable in their cruelty, depraved beyond belief, were recruited to administer these extermination centres.

Below: ***Former inmates of the death camps show the identity numbers tattooed on their arms by the Nazis.***

Below, right: ***A synagogue in ruins after the attacks against Jews during Crystal Night, 9 November, 1938.***

Such a man was Rudolf Hoess, commandant of Auschwitz where the final solution was to reach remarkable heights of cruel efficiency. Hoess, at his peak, oversaw a complex where men and women lived in filth, were worked like dogs and finally executed when they were no longer of any use to the Reich. Auschwitz, and its annexe camp of Birkenau, where the gas chambers and crematorium were situated, were two miles from the main town of the same name in southern Poland. Every day, in the camps, twelve thousand people died in the gas chambers before being burned in the massive crematorium.

Hoess took a scientific delight in solving the problems of mass murder. Auschwitz, like the other camps, had used mass shootings and hangings to eradicate the inmates, but this was precisely the inefficiency that Hitler and the SS wanted to do away with. Later in 1942 a gas made from prussic acid. that was used to kill rats and mice in German factories, was deployed for the first time against Russian POWs. The Russians were led into a long, sealed room, the walls of which were lined with showers. But the shower faucets were false and the plugholes sealed. And then they heard the rattle of hard crystals dropped on to a wire grating above their heads, before the room filled with a gas, called Zyklon-B, that was released from the crystals. They were all dead within twenty minutes.

At the far south end of the Birkenau camp two massive gas chambers and adjacent crematoriums were built by the inmates themselves. Trains arriving at a railhead were greeted by one Dr Josef Mengele – about whom more will be said later – the SS doctor who became supreme arbiter of life and death within the electrified fences of Auschwitz. With a flick of his riding crop he dictated the fate of the inmates. Those who were to work for the Reich on starvation rations, under the blows of whips and cudgels, marched one way while their elderly parents, sisters brothers, and toddlers walked the other.

Loudspeakers told the latter group that they were heading off for showers and delousing before they were to be re-united with their families in barracks. In fact, they were taken to a long wooden hut where they were told to strip and place all valuables in a locker. Then their heads were shaved and the hair collected in giant sacks by other prisoners. Then they were marched in to the giant shower-rooms. But these showers did not flow with water and the naked humiliated prisoners were actually in giant death chambers

BODILY REMAINS

Afterwards, men working for the *Sonderkommando* or special commando squads set up by their SS overlords, entered to disentangle the corpses and remove the gold fillings from their teeth. The bodies were then pushed into the ovens, the ashes raked out and spread over nearby woodland or dumped in the River Vistula.

Cruel and inhuman as the killing machine was, death was often the one thing the living prayed for. The camp culture spawned a sadistic, warped race of guards who took morbid pleasure in the mistreatment of their charges. Irma Greese, the 'Blonde Angel of Hell' from Belsen, delighted in flaying women's breasts with a knotted whip. Karl Babor, the camp doctor of the Gross-Rosen camp, amused himself by burning new-born babies on an open fire. And at Auschwitz there was the infamous Dr Mengele, whose smiling face was always there to greet the new arrivals as they arived in stinking cattle wagons.

Mengele was a doctor of medicine who betrayed his Hippocratic oath each and every day, while convincing himself that his scientific research in the camp was carried out on mere 'subhumans'.

His greetings at the train ramp for the Auschwitz arrivals had a dual purpose; he sorted out those who could work for the Reich before their deaths, and he sought blue-eyed twins so he could perform experiments aimed at cloning the Nordic supermen which Hitler had decreed were to be the new chosen race. And all the while he salved the shreds of his wicked conscience by claiming that *he* was saving life for the future! Yet all experts concur that on his personal orders alone some four hundred thousand Jews were executed. Prisoners, infected with lice, TB, typhus, typhoid and grotesque medieval-style infections – infections bred by the poor diet and insanitary conditions which prevailed in the camps – existed in a twilight zone of brutality that could only be eased by death. When they were no longer able to function in the armaments plants and quarries adjacent to the camps they were eliminated. The gold teeth from the corpses were sent to the Reichsbank in Berlin, their hair was

Below, left: ***Inmates were used to clear away the bodies of their fellow prisoners and feed them into the crematoriums of the death camps.***

Below: ***Hitler with his mistress, Eva Braun, relaxes in his mountain retreat at Berchtesgaden.***

Left: ***Those destined for the concentration camps were packed into cattle trucks for the journey.***

Below: ***Grim photographs are both proof of, and constant reminders of, the barbaric slaughter of millions of innocent Europeans in the Nazi camps.***

used to stuff mattresses for troops on the Russian front and the fat from their bodies was processed into soap. Such was the efficiency that Adolf Hitler demanded and got from his loyal servants of evil.

Adolf Eichmann, like Mengele, was a classic product of the twisted logic of Nazism. He saw no evil in what he was doing, believed that he was a 'good soldier' who was only obeying orders. Day after day, as Germany was losing the war on all fronts, this son of an accountant re-routed armaments trains headed for the troops with supplies and rations, and cancelled returning hospital trains, so he could use the rolling stock to clear out the ghettoes of Eastern Europe and thus feed the furnaces at the extermination camps. But he was not flamboyant, more a grey bureaucrat and his cruelty only became public after the collapse of the Reich in May 1945.

During the height of the Holocaust one thousand trains a week were criss-crossing Europe with people destined for the camps. In the middle of 1943 fully a third of all camp inmates assigned to work details died each week. Survival became a matter of co-operating with the SS – by getting a job in a camp clinic, becoming a block captain, seizing any chance to please the SS – anything that might bring a chance of survival. The overwhelming horror of these places was belied by the cynical slogan Himmler placed above the entrance gates of the camps – *Arbeit Macht Frei* – Work Brings Freedom. It was a bitter lie.

Not the campswere not the only disgrace. As brave German soldiers fought valiantly at places like Stalingrad and Kharkhov, the *Einsatzgruppen* squads were forever besmirching Germany's name with their mass executions. Herman Graebe, a German civilian engineer working on road-building in the Ukraine, witnessed just such

HIMMLER PLACED ABOVE THE ENTRANCE GATES OF THE CAMPS – *ARBEIT MACHT FREI* – WORK BRINGS FREEDOM.

Above: ***Allied soldiers guard captured Nazi leaders during the massive war crimes trial held in Nurnberg after the defeat of Nazi Germany***

Right: ***Adolf Eichmann was finally captured in the Sixties. He pleaded his cause before a weary Judge Moishe Landau (far right).***

Opposite, far right: ***Herman Goering in prison, awaiting sentence, during the war crimes trial.***

'WITHOUT SCREAMING OR WEEPING THESE PEOPLE UNDRESSED, STOOD AROUND IN FAMILY GROUPS, KISSED EACH OTHER, SAID FAREWELLS, AND WAITED FOR THE SIGN FROM THE SS MAN WHO STOOD BESIDE THE PIT.

a scene. He wrote: 'Without screaming or weeping these people undressed, stood around in family groups, kissed each other, said farewells, and waited for the sign from the SS man who stood beside the pit with a whip in his hand. During the fifteen minutes I stood near, I heard no complaint or plea for mercy. I watched a family... An old woman with snow-white hair was holding a child of about one in her arms, singing to it and tickling it. The child was cooing with delight. The parents were looking on with tears in their eyes. The father was holding the hand of a boy about

ten years old and speaking to him softly; the boy was fighting back tears. The father pointed to the sky, stroked his head and seemed to explain something to him.

'At that moment the SS man at the pit started shouting something to his comrade. The comrade counted off about twenty people and instructed them to go behind the earth mound. Among them was the family I have just mentioned. I well remember a slim girl with black hair who, as she passed me, pointed to herself and said: 'Twenty-three'. I walked around the mound and stood in front of a tremendous grave. People were closely wedged together and lying on top of each other so that only their heads were visible. Nearly all had blood running over their shoulders from their heads. Some were lifting their heads and moving their arms to show that they were still alive. The pit was nearly two-thirds full and I estimated that it contained about one thousand people. I looked at the man who did the shooting. He was an SS man who sat at the edge of the narrow end of the pit, his feet dangling into it. He had a tommy-gun on his knees and was smoking a cigarette. The people, completely naked, went down some steps which were cut in the clay wall of the pit and clambered over the heads of the people lying there, to the place to which the SS man directed them. Some caressed those who were still alive and spoke to them in low voices.'

Above: ***A rogues' gallery of Nazis. From the left, Propaganda minister, Goebbels; SS Chief, Himmler; Deputy Hess and Hitler, all together at a pre-War rally.***

A DIGNITY IN DEATH

Towards the end of the war the Nazis increased their frantic efforts to wipe out the estimated nine million Jews within the conquered lands. One of Eichmann's greatest coups in the desperate days of 1944, as the Russians were advancing rapidly throughout Eastern Europe, was to get the Hungarians to hand over half of their population of eight hundred thousand Jews. They were all gassed at Auschwitz – an achievement which Eichmann said gave him 'intense satisfaction'.

Most Jews and other Nazi victims went nobly and quietly to their deaths. They had a dignity which mocked the brutality of their tormentors, yet the Nazis liked to crow that the Jews had continually shown their weakness in life's struggle because they did not fight, but meekly submitted to the sword. But in reality, there was nowhere for these tortured people to go if they had escaped, no prospect of victory over well-trained and well-fed guards.

The Nazis did not have it entirely their own way. At Sachsenhausen many guards were killed in an armed breakout and, in 1944, the Jewish Underground in Auschwitz placed explosives in one of the ovens and blew it to smithereens. The most impressive display of defiance came when Hitler ordered the destruction of the Warsaw Ghetto in 1944. Here, the Jews of Poland were housed, but they refused to be taken to the trains and, with smuggled weaponry, killed SS men.

It took half-a-division of SS men with full anti-tank and armour facilities to rout the defenders in four months of bitter fighting. It cost the Jews fifty-six thousand lives and kept valuable German soldiers away from the fight on the front. Such were the twisted values of Nazism – the defenceless Jew always considered more of an enemy than guns, tanks and armed soldiers.

While they may have salved their own consciences about what took place in the death camps, with the excuse that they were 'only obeying orders', the guilty men

In the west, it was the Americans and the British who liberated the Nazi charnel houses of Belsen and Buchenwald.

Josef Kramer, the commandant of Belsen, was puzzled by the fury of the ordinary British squaddies who liberated his fiefdom; could not understand why they were so belligerent towards him. At his

'I didn't feel anything towards the prisoners. I received orders to kill them and that's what I did. Surely you cannot expect a soldier in wartime to disobey an order?'

Left: ***His charm and determination gave Adolf Hitler a terrible power over a nation broken by their defeat in the Great War.***

Below: ***A unique picture of Jews arriving from a train at the Czech concentration camp of Terezin.***

knew what awaited them. Auschwitz personnel fled the camp just twenty-four hours before Russian troops arrived to liberate the wretches left inside. The air was still heavy with the sickly-sweet stench of burned human flesh and the crematorium, the one that was still working, had corpses awaiting burning. In a warehouse barracks that the Nazis dubbed 'Canada' because of its vast size, the Russians found a mountain of human hair, gold teeth, underwear, clothing and jewellery – the last destined for the Reichsbank. Hoess had planned to demolish Auschwitz but he left it too late. But Franz Stangl, commandant of Treblinka, managed to destroy his camp. The only testimonies to its existence are the tracks of the railway line, and the deep green hue of the grass over the rich, fertile ground that, in places, is twelve feet thick with human bonemeal.

from Swiss banks the names of wealthy Jewish clients, now used the same good offices of secrecy for their own flight.

REFUGE FOR THE WICKED

South America, where military regimes had long expressed solidarity and sympathy with the Nazi cause, was a favourite destination. Eichmann headed for Argentina; Mengele for Brazil; Joseph Schwammberger, commandant of the concentration camp at Przemysl, to Argentina; Alois Brunner, designer of the mobile gas-wagons and the brains behind the deportation of forty-six thousand Greek Jews to Auschwitz, made it to Damascus where he still lives under Arab protection.

Justice for those left behind was swift; many camp guards were executed within days of liberation. The Nuremberg trials despatched many more, including Kramer and Greese. But it was left to people like Simon Wiesenthal, who lost eighty members of his family in the Holocaust, to become the conscience of the world – to ensure that mankind never forgot what revolting crimes had taken place.

Wiesenthal is an old man now, his shoulders slightly hunched and his hair grey, but his eyes have lost none of their fire. He survived the death camps and has pledged his life to tracking down Nazi war criminals and bringing them to justice. His determination and diligence led to the capture of Eichmann in Argentina and the deportation from South America of Lyons Gestapo chief Klaus Barbie.

Weisenthal's small office in central Vienna is called the Documentation Centre and it is a museum to the memory of the slain. Wiesenthal calculates that as many as fourteen million were claimed by the Nazis in their war of racial purification. From 22 March, 1933, when Dachau, twelve miles from Munich, opened as the Reich's first concentration camp, until the Allies liberated the entire network, Hitler had managed to dispose of over a third of Europe's Jews. Wiesenthal inflates his figures because of the special 'actions' undertaken in Russia, the enormity of which has still to be fully understood.

Even now Weisenthal is still hunting, still ceaselessly bringing to justice those who perpetrated mankind's biggest mass

trial after the war for his crimes at the Natzweiler, Auschwitz and Belsen camps, he told those judging him: 'I didn't feel anything towards the prisoners. I received orders to kill them and that's what I did. Surely you cannot expect a soldier in wartime to disobey an order?'

But Kramer and all the others – Babor of Gross-Rosen, Mengele of Auschwitz, Heinrich 'Gestapo' Mueller, Adolf Eichmann, Franz Stangl of Treblinka – all tried to escape. They knew that their blind obedience to orders would never stand up in a courtroom whose loyalty was not to Adolf Hitler. Using the services of the ODESSA – the Organization of Former Members of the SS – they drew on secret Swiss bank accounts to pay for new identities and lives in distant lands. Much of the money came from the victims whose butchery they had overseen in the camps. It was a final bitter twist of irony that the SS who had tried, without success, to wheedle

Above: ***The power-mad, ruthless Herman Goering started the Gestapo to enforce the more ruthless aspects of Nazi rule.***

Opposite, top: ***The Nazis sought to whip up anti-semitic feelings with crude caricatures meant to persaude citizens that the Jews were untrustworthy.***

Opposite, below: ***Gold was extracted from the teeth of concentration camp victims. The gold was boxed and delivered to the Reichsbank.***

murder. He cannot stop, not while revisionist historians and neo-Nazi sympathisers, now on the rise in Europe and Russia, are busy denying that the Holocaust with its death camps ever happened.

Wiesenthal would die a happy man if he could get Alois Brunner, the committed Nazi, who, in 1965, said to reporters from a German newspaper: 'I'm glad! I'm proud of what I did. If I could have fed more Yids into the flame I would. I don't regret a thing – we were only destroying vermin.'

Simon Wiesenthal finds some solace in the report he will give to the Lord when it is his time to depart. this life

'We will all be called before the Lord for judgement,' he said, 'and we will be asked to give an account of ourselves. One man will say: "I became a tailor". Another will say: "I became a doctor". Yet another will say: "I became a jeweller".

'And I will be able to say: "I did not forget you...".'

SADDAM HUSSEIN
Genocide of the Kurds

The proud warrior tribes refused to bend before a dictator. So he took his vicious revenge. He sprayed them with terrible chemicals, which brought painful and dreadful death to thousands of Kurdish men, women and children.

Long before the high-tech war visited on his country by the Allied forces during Operation Desert Storm, Iraqi despot Saddam Hussein had waged another, dirtier kind of war within his own borders. His enemy was the fiercely proud Kurdish tribe, the hot-blooded warrior race that, for centuries, has longed for an independent Kurdistan that would span the border between Iraqi and Turkey.

Hussein assembled one of the greatest war machines ever seen, before it was dismantled during the Gulf War. In manpower alone, he had the fifth largest army in the world, plus a formidable array of conventional and chemical weaponry. He needed to ensure that he was the master of the Middle East, but part of his arsenal was developed for a plan every bit as sinister as that hatched by the Nazis. He wanted to wipe out the Kurdish people once and for all. In 1988, before his power was stunted, if not altogether broken by the West, Saddam unleashed his appalling chemical weapons against innocent Kurds, as part of his blueprint for their destruction, killing over four thousand people. Against his arch-enemy Iran, whom he fought for eight futile years, he used mustard gas.

His chemical weapons programme was one of the most advanced in the world. America and the former USSR had long ago curbed production of chemical weapons, which are forbidden under United Nations rulings and the Geneva Convention. The world did not want to repeat the horrors of the First World War where chemical weapons had been used. But Saddam, who does not yet have nuclear power, realised that massive stockpiles of lethal gas would give him a huge military advantage over his enemies.

The technology has not changed a great deal in the years since the Great War – the poison is still delivered by shell and bomb – but the chemical content has. Saddam developed hydrogen cyanide, a particularly lethal gas which causes death within two seconds when inhaled. He also developed new versions of the nerve gases Tabun and Sarun, pioneered by the Nazis during the Second World War, though never used by them. A very small quantity of either of these gases, will, when it falls on skin, cause a human being to go into convulsions, followed very quickly by death.

HUSSEIN ASSEMBLED ONE OF THE GREATEST WAR MACHINES EVER SEEN, BEFORE IT WAS DISMANTLED DURING THE GULF WAR.

Opposite: ***Saddam Hussein, the butcher of Baghdad. He is feared because of his ruthless quest for power in the Middle East.***

THE MEANS OF DESTRUCTION

The technology needed for his gas programme was provided by the Western nations that would one day be arrayed against him. As long as Saddam Hussein was keeping the forces of Islamic fundamentalism on the opposite bank of the Euphrates River, the West was happy to give him the means for mass destruction. Western companies salved their consciences by saying that much of the hardware necessary for the production of chemical warfare was for fertilizer factories

Above: ***Refugees wend their way to Piranshar in Iran to escape the persecution of Saddam Hussein in Iraq.***

within Iraq, although any scientist knows that it is but a small step from producing fertilizers to poison gas. Some were merely duped. The Phillips Petroleum Company of Bartlesville, Ohio, was one of the American companies whose security system failed it. Phillips, through a Belgian unit, had sold the Iraqis five hundred tons of a complex chemical called thiodiglycol, believing it was for use as a fertilizer. Combined with hydrochloric acid, it makes mustard gas. An understanding of what had been made from their shipment to Saddam hit company executives, when in 1988, they read news reports of Iranian soldiers on a remote battlefield coughing up their lungs, and of corpses covered with horrifying chemical burns.

Germany, Holland and Britain also sold chemical weapon technology and raw materials to Iraq, enabling Saddam to build up stockpiles which sent shivers through his bitterest enemy – Israel. Israel, long before Saddam unleashed his Scud missiles on her cities during the Gulf War, feared a pre-emptive strike with chemical missiles.

When Saddam used his mustard gas on the battlefield, it was in limited quantities and aimed strategically at Iranian command posts and communications centres; rarely was it used against civilians. But in his war against the Kurds he had no such qualms.

The Kurds were, and still are, Saddam Hussein's biggest political problem. They are not impressed by his bellicose speeches, the huge pictures of him that adorn public buildings and stretch over highways; nor do they pay anything other than lip-service to his regime. The Kurds, armed and virtually autonomous in the northern, mountainous region of Iraq were to be taught a tragic, final lesson that they would never be able to forget.

In March 1988, while the war against Iran was still raging, Saddam received reports from his battlefront commanders that Iranian troops, aided by Kurdish guerillas, had seized control of the Kurdish town of Halabja. The town was based near a vital hydro-electric dam. The information that Iranian troops were involved gave Saddam reason to unleash his deadliest poisons on the innocent civilian population. Yet he must have known that there were, in fact, no Iranian troops in the town because they left within hours of taking it.

Above: ***A tent city, housing thousands of refugees, has arisen on the Turkish border as people flee the repression of Iraq.***

THE DEADLY CLOUD

The sun was just rising over the mountain peaks when the first shells began to rain down on Halabja. But unlike the high explosives that the citizens had heard falling along the battlefront with Iran, there was only a soft 'plop-plopping' as the shells dropped without detonating. But soon palls of sickly yellow, white and grey gas began to swell and swirl, drifting like fog through the streets, creeping into every nook and cranny. Saddam had uncorked his evil weapons of Tabun, cyanide gas and mustard gas on the townspeople. Chaos and hysteria reigned as panic gripped the

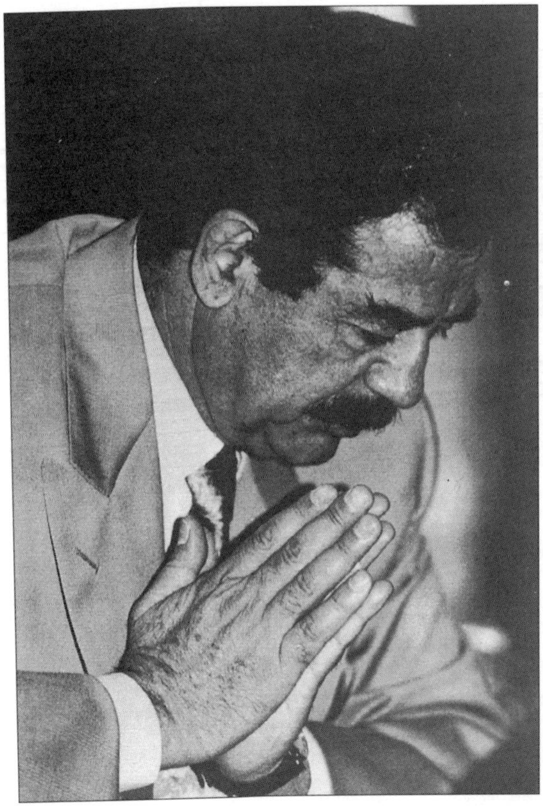

townsfolk. They ran through the streets, their skin peeling from their faces when the mustard-sulphur clouds hit them. If they ran into Tabun fumes, they were dead within seconds. A shocking photograph recorded a poignant death during this morning of carnage. It shows a mother clutching her dead baby in the main street, both killed as they ran in a frantic attempt to seek cover from the deadly clouds.

By the afternoon the donkeys and goats in the fields were all dead, the vegetation wilted. The sickly smell of rotten onion mixed with burned garlic hung over the air. It was as if someone had gone in with a giant fly spray and snuffed out the life of all the citizens. Only those who had been working in remote fields survived. In all, four thousand men, women and children died on that tragic day in Halabja.

Caglayan Cugen, a Turkish doctor who treated survivors who had burns and respiratory problems, said: 'They talked of seeing these blue canisters from which the gas came. There was an odd odour first and then they remember burning in their eyes, blurring the vision as the eyes smart and itch. There followed uncontrollable bouts of sneezing and vomiting. Their breath shortens in the hours following inhalation of the mustard gas as the inflammation spreads, swelling the internal lining. Many of them had horrible blisters on their necks, chests and thighs, causing huge patches of skin to fall off. Large lesions broke out over their genital areas. They were young and old but they were not soldiers. The youngest I treated was a baby of four months. I could not help but ask what they had done to deserve this.'

Iraq, usually so adept at controlling press coverage within its borders, made the mistake of allowing Western newsmen and foreign relief workers into the area. The pictures of thousands of bodies without any visible wounds whatsoever belied Bagdhad's statement that they had been killed in the cross-fire of shelling between the forces of Iraq and Iran. It was several months before the Iranian leadership admitted to the use of the gas as 'a necessary measure to drive out the Iranian infidels'.

BUT SOON PALLS OF SICKLY YELLOW, WHITE AND GREY GAS BEGAN TO SWELL AND SWIRL, DRIFTING LIKE FOG THROUGH THE STREETS.

Left: ***Hussein may not be a good man, but he is a devout one.***

Below: ***Iranian soldiers cower in their trenches during the war against Iraq.***

Above: ***Mustard gas killed this woman and her baby during a chemical warfare assault against Kurds in the town of Halabja.***

A UN official who saw the carnage said: 'The bodies were lying in doorways, in streets, around tables set up for lunch and in cellars where people mistakenly sought shelter from the heavier-than-air gas. Many other corpses were found on the roads leading from the town, where residents had failed to outrun the spreading cloud. The victims seemed to have died quickly, as there were few signs of a struggle. The streets were also littered with the bloated carcasses of cows, dogs, cats, sheep and goats.

A TERRIBLE OUTRAGE

'Some thirty of the victims were flown for treatment at hospitals in the West, which confirmed that several poison gas agents were indeed deployed on the innocent civilians. Iranian doctors I spoke with, who treated those refugees who managed to cross over into their country, said their tests had shown that the gases were mustard, cyanide and nerve gas. The injured suffered from the most appalling burns and their lungs were all but destroyed.'

'DESPITE THE FACT THAT SADDAM HUSSEIN COMMITTED MAJOR ACTS OF GENOCIDE, THE FACT IS, IRAQ GOT AWAY WITH IT.'

Western diplomats in Iraq were appalled at the outrage. 'Halabja was inexcuseable in every sense of the word,' said one indignant emissary at the time. 'The use of poison gas against enemy troops is bad enough, but to use it against civilians, and especially your own citizens, is quite unbelieveable.'

Steven Rose, a neurobiologist at Britain's Open University, said: 'Despite the fact that Saddam Hussein committed major acts of genocide, the fact is, Iraq got away with it.' There was no pressure to bring this criminal, a man who clearly and openly violated the rules of war, to justice. No less than six separate United Nations missions went to Iraq before and after the Halabja massacre, each time collecting more information on Iraqi chemical assaults. One team was despatched to the town of Halabja and reported: 'This warns us that the use of chemical weapons against the Kurdish people may become more frequent, even commonplace.'

Saddam was well satisfied with this awesome display of his maniacal power. He had cocked a snook at world opinon, defied

Above: ***Western newsmen recorded the murder of Kurds in the streets of Halabja.***

Left: ***A frantic and terrified people trekked great distances to reach the safety of Turkey.***

the conventions of the West – which he viewed as weak – and had dealt a stunning blow to his Kurdish enemies. He felt so good about it that he decided to do it again.

TWO BLEEDING NATIONS

In August 1988 the guns finally fell silent in his war with Iran. It had bled the two nations white, ravaged their economies, decimated their populations and cemented the politics of hate for generations to come. But the onset of peace for Saddam meant he could turn more manpower – and more chemical weaponry – against his Kurdish foes.

By the end of August Saddam had moved some sixty thousand troops into the Kurdish region, together with battalions of

'IT IS ONE THING TO BE BLOWN TO PIECES, BUT IT IS ANOTHER TO BE KILLED BY A WEAPON YOU CANNOT HEAR AND CANNOT SEE UNTIL IT IS TOO LATE.'

SEFIKA ALI IS NOW TWENTY-FOUR, BUT HER PRETTY FACE IS WRINKLED LIKE THAT OF A MUCH OLDER WOMAN. THIS IS THE RESULT OF CYANIDE GAS BURNS.

Right: ***The presence of their despot cannot be forgotten by the Iraqi people. His image looms on billboards across the country.***

helicopter gunships, tanks and artillery; all effective methods of launching the gas blitz he intended. The first village to die under his onslaught was Butia.

Sefika Ali is now twenty-four, but her pretty face is wrinkled like that of a much older woman. This is the result of cyanide gas burns which happened when her village was wiped out in a gas attack launched from the air. She fled to Turkey with her husband and three children. They were the lucky ones. Left behind were an estimated two thousand neighbours, who suffered the same death as the victims of Halabja. She said: 'I was cooking breakfast for my family when I heard the sound of aircraft. I heard bombs whistling and the next thing I knew was that there was something wrong with my eyes. I started to vomit almost immediately. I knew what was happening. We had heard what had happened at Halabja. My family suffered the same effects. We all drank a lot of milk and then we ran. We ran to get as far away as we could. We know that not many made it out.'

REFUGEES FACING DEATH

In the refugee camps along the Turkish border the hordes of burned, coughing survivors of the latest outrage swelled the hospital tents as medical teams from the West struggled to cope with the aftermath of Saddam's attacks. The refugees were called *Pesh mergas* by the Iraqis – 'Those who face death' – and there were no apologies from Bagdhad for the fate of these victims. It was estimated that along with Butia, two other villages in the Danhuk region of the country were hit, but these suffered few fatalities because the populace were working in far-away fields and strong winds blowing that morning helped disperse the gas away from them.

Kurdish refugees, almost one hundred thousand of them, moved into Turkey, where they were accommodated in insanitary, overcrowded tented camps along the border. Massad Barzani, one of the Kurdish leaders, appealed to the UN to press Iraq not to use any more chemical weapons. He said: 'It is one thing to be blown to pieces, but it is another to be killed by a weapon you cannot hear and cannot see until it is too late. In the name of humanity, the governments of the west must come together to end this nightmare we are suffering. Many women and children who were gassed, but who survived the onslaught were later murdered by Iraqi troops to prevent them from spreading information about what dark deeds were done to them. It is a crime against humanity we are talking about here.'

In September the Reagan administration in America finally woke up to the atrocities, realising that Saddam Hussein was becoming more of a liability than an ally in the region. On 8 September, the State Department said it had obtained proof of the latest outrages and called them abhorrent and unjustifiable. Secretary of State George Shultz met with Iraqi's Minister of State for Foreign Affairs, Saddoun Hammadi, to tell him that the continued use of poison gas would severely affect the future of US - Iraq relations.

Hammadi insisted, despite all the evidence to the contrary, that no civilians had this time been killed by gas. Gwynne Roberts, a British television journalist, had himself collected soil samples from some of the villages he visited in Kurdistan and had them analysed by a laboratory. The laboratory report showed significant traces of mustard gas in the samples.

The anger felt by Shultz and other officials was supported by the American people and there was a popular feeling that maybe America had, after all, been backing the wrong horse in the long struggle between Iran and Iraq. Senator Claiborne Pell, a Democrat from Rhode Island, introduced a bill calling for sanctions against Iraq for what he called its 'anti-Kurdish genocide'. There was a period of an arms embargo after more UN evidence of the chemical atrocities was revealed, but sadly trade soon resumed again.

Below: ***The strange dual role played by Saddam Hussein is revealed in this photograph: the militant warrior is also a pious man of God.***

ALFREDO ASTIZ
The Dirty war

The new military government promised to return Argentina to its former glory. Instead, they unleashed a gang of sadists upon the nation – men like Astiz who led a dirty war of murder and torture against his own people.

Between 1976 and 1982 Argentina waged a full-scale war within its own borders. The enemy were classified as those who acted or sympathised with anyone who had a viewpoint other than that espoused by the government. The military junta in power called their reign of terror The Process of National Reorganization. But it was a fancy euphemism for mass murder, whereby people vanished into human slaughterhouses, were tortured there and murdered. Coffee-bar socialists, mothers of radicals, babies of dissidents, long-lost cousins of intellectuals who had once read a Communist pamphlet – these were the victims of this 'Process' known to the rest of the world as the 'Dirty War'. And working within this state terror machine were individuals like Lt Alfredo Astiz.

THE CLEANSING OF SOCIETY

Astiz was a member of the officer corps which took upon itself the burden of 'cleansing' Argentinian society. The military throughout South America has had a long and shameful history of interference in civilian governments but none more so than the Argentinian army. Military rule has dominated Argentina and between 1930 and 1982, the only civilian government to last its full term was that of Juan Peron. For years, after no less than six coups, the men in uniform guided – or rather, misguided – the fortunes of this land rich in minerals, farming and cattle.

When the sophisticated and cosmopolitan citizens of Buenos Aries woke up to the clatter of tank tracks on the cobbled streets of their gracious city on 23 March, 1976 they did not panic; they had, after all, heard and seen it all before.

This time, it was a General Jorge Videla telling the people that massive unemployment, inflation running at eight hundred per cent and a resurgence of left-wing violence had driven the military to grab power. Videla, having seized the radio and television stations, put it to his people like this: 'Since all constitutional mechanisms have been exhausted, and since the impossibility of recovery through normal processes has been irrefutably demonstrated, the armed forces must put an end to this situation which has burdened the nation. This government will be imbued with a profound national spirit, and will respond only to the most sacred interests of the nation and its inhabitants.'

THIS GOVERNMENT WILL BE IMBUED WITH A PROFOUND NATIONAL SPIRIT.

Above: ***The Mothers of the Plaza de Mayo defied arrest, torture and even death as they paraded before the junta headquarters in frequent mass demands for the return of their children.***

Opposite: ***The raffish, handsome exterior of naval officer, Alfredo Astiz, hid the ugly torturer of the death squads.***

There was a tone of determination in his voice which made the people of Argentina embrace rather than shrink from military government. Leftist guerillas had, since 1966, been rampant in the countryside, murdering, kidnapping, committing atrocities among the civil population. The country was on an inexorable slide into anarchy as it battled against these guerilla groups, most notably the *Ejercito*

Above: ***Dagmar Hagelin, a young Swedish woman, disappeared after the junta kidnapped her.***

Opposite, top: ***Alfredo Astiz enters the court where he faced charges regarding the disappearance of Dagmar Hagelin.***

Opposite, below: ***Ragnar Hagelin stands outside the military court after he was notified of the acquittal of Astiz who was charged with the disappearance of Hagelin's daughter.***

Revolucionarioa del Pueblo – People's Revolutionary Army – and the *Montoneros*. There is a school of thought which says that, had these terrorists not created a climate of fear which brought the army out of its barracks and put the torturers in government, fifteen thousand innocent people might still be alive today. But Videla and his henchmen were welcomed by a tired population who were glad to listen to his ideas on The Process of National Reorganization.

While Videla uttered platitudes and told his own people, and the world at large, that his government would respect human rights, his machinery of terror was being secretly assembled, soon to be unleashed on an unsuspecting population.

The officer corps of the Argentinian armed forces saw themselves as an elite group, imbued with the national spirit as no other body within Argentina. Many proved very happy to oversee the terror required to reorganize their countrymen, but none more so than Alfredo Astiz, who was to develop into an infamous torturer, his name forever linked with this shameful period of Argentina's sad history.

THE DEATH SQUADS

Astiz, a handsome naval lieutenant of wealthy parents, drank deeply from the poisoned chalice offered by Videla. He believed the General when he said that the enemies of Argentina were within its own frontiers. With the zeal of a Spanish Inquisition cardinal, Astiz helped enthusiastically in the founding and operation of ESMA, the Navy Mechanics School in Buenos Aries, which was nothing more than a human abbatoir hiding behind the name of an institute of marine engineering.

Thousands of victims of 'The Process' were brought as prisoners to the Navy Mechanics School where they were subjected to the most horrific beatings and torture, then taken out for execution; very few made it back to families and loved ones. It was not only the navy that organized this kind of torture centre; the army, air force and police were also involved, each one vying for glory as they hunted the 'enemy within'. They operated in squads called *patotas* and they each found places to turn into centres of hell, where they dragged the dissidents who, they believed, were destroying the Argentinian way of life and its cultural traditions.

One of the few victims to survive after Astiz and his men had captured her has a horrifying story to tell. Twenty-seven-year-old nursery school teacher Isabel Gamba de Negrotti was pregnant when she was seized at gunpoint by the *patotas* and taken away in a green Ford Falcon car – a make of car that came to be indelibly linked with death – and dumped in the Navy Mechanics School. The young woman described her ordeal: 'They took me to a room after arrival where they kicked me and punched me in the head. Then they undressed me and beat me on the legs, buttocks and shoulders with something made of rubber. This lasted a long time. I fell down several times and they made me stand by supporting myself on a table... While all this was going on they talked to me, insulted me, and asked me about people I didn't know and things I didn't understand.

The junta was going after the children, the students and the trade unionists, the journalists and the teachers – all were swept up in the vortex of terror. Victims were picked up at random and, as these citizens were bundled into the death cars, they would yell out their names and addresses to passers-by who, in turn, would inform families that their relations had joined *los desparecidos* – 'the disappeared'.

Often the military disposed of their victims by pushing bodies, dead or alive, out of helicopters as they flew over rivers. Almost five thousand people are believed to have met their deaths on these 'NN' – 'No-Name' – flights. Others were buried in mass graves on the pampas or in remote corners of country churchyards, buried without name, sacrament or ceremony.

Inside the Navy Mechanics School, Astiz and other torturers preferred even crueller forms of death and practised bizarre forms of torture and sadism against men, women and children.

Many people who came across Astiz compared him to Dr Josef Mengele, the Nazi death camp doctor at Auschwitz. Astiz who was fair-haired and blue-eyed,

'I pleaded with them to leave me alone, otherwise I would lose my baby. I hadn't the strength to speak, the pain was so bad. They started to give me electric shocks on my breasts, the side of my body and under my arms. They kept questioning me. They gave me electric shocks in the vagina and put a pillow over my mouth to stop me screaming. Someone called 'The Colonel' came and said they were going to increase the voltage until I talked, but I didn't know what they wanted me to talk about. They kept throwing water over my body and applying electric shocks all over. Two days later I miscarried.' She survived the ordeal.

Enemies real and imagined were seen everywhere by officers of the junta. Their paranoia is revealed in a telling comment from Fifth Army Corps Commander General Adel Vilas, that he made some months after 'The Process' had started: 'Up to now only the tip of the iceberg has been affected by our war against subversion... it is necessary to destroy the sources which feed, form and indoctrinate the subversive delinquent, and the source is the universities and secondary schools themselves.'

OFTEN THE MILITARY DISPOSED OF THEIR VICTIMS BY PUSHING BODIES, DEAD OR ALIVE, OUT OF HELICOPTERS AS THEY FLEW OVER RIVERS.

THEY ROAMED AT WILL, AT ANY HOUR OF THE DAY OR NIGHT, SATISFYING WHATEVER GROTESQUE LUSTS CAME UPON THEM WITH ANY VICTIM THEY HAPPENED UPON.

SOMEONE CALLED 'THE COLONEL' CAME AND SAID THEY WERE GOING TO INCREASE THE VOLTAGE UNTIL I TALKED, BUT I DIDN'T KNOW WHAT THEY WANTED ME TO TALK ABOUT.

was nicknamed 'the blonde angel' and he revelled in his sadistic work. He was keen from the very beginning of 'The Process' to take on the dirty, murderous tasks that many of his naval comrades refused.

Raul Vilarano, the killer who later confessed to the horrible deeds perpetrated by himself and Astiz, said that he and his cohorts did not work to any pattern at the Navy Mechanics School; rather, they roamed at will, at any hour of the day or night, satisfying whatever grotesque lusts came upon them with any victim they happened upon. Dagmar Hagelin happened to be one of those victims.

Dagmar was arrested on 27 January, 1977. She had Swedish nationality even though she was raised in Argentina, and

Right: ***These men of the Junta faced murder charges. Clockwise: Jorge Videla, Emilio Massera, Orlando Agosti, Omar Graffigna, Basilio Lami Dozo, Jorge Anaya, Leopoldo Galtieri, Roberta Viola and, centre, Armando Lambruschini.***

Opposite: ***Alfredo Astiz in his role as naval officer signs his surrender to the British during the Falklands War, and in the lower picture, he goes to court as a suspected criminal to face charges of kidnap and murder.***

was a gifted eighteen-year-old classical music student with coffee-table ideas about socialism, but no affiliation with any guerilla groups or other Communist subversives. As she rang the bell at a friend's house two men – a *patota* squad from the Navy Mechanics School – appeared and Dagmar ran, only to be shot down in the street. She was dumped in the boot of a Ford Falcon and driven away. The man who had fired the shot was Astiz.

Unlike other 'no-names' who had disappeared, Dagmar did not come from the poor and powerless. Her father ran a profitable business and was on good terms with the Swedish ambassador but, though he used every influence to trace his daughter, his efforts were to no avail. Dagmar, another innocent among thousands, died in the Navy Mechanics School and her remains have never been found. The Swedish ambassador refused to accept honours from his host country when it came time for him to take up another diplomatic posting – he did not want to give credence to a regime that, he was convinced, murdered young girls.

Jacobo Timerman, a Jewish newspaper editor who was deemed sympathetic to the enemies of the state, was tortured by Astiz but he survived to shame the military men with an account of his suffering in the book 'Prisoner Without a Name, Cell Without a Number'. He wrote: 'When electric shocks are applied, all that a man feels is that they're ripping his flesh apart. And he howls. Afterwards, he doesn't feel the blows. Nor does he feel them the next day, when there's no electricity, but only blows. The man spends days confined in a cell without windows, without light, either seated or lying down. The man spends a month without being allowed to wash himself, transported on the floor of an automobile to various places of interrogation, fed badly, smelling bad. The man is left enclosed in a small cell for forty-eight hours, his eyes blindfolded, his hands tied behind him, hearing no voice, seeing no sign of life, having to perform his bodily

functions upon himself. And there is not much more. Objectively, nothing more.'

Astiz reached new heights of cynicism and cruelty when he posed as Gustavo Nino, a peasant boy who had lost relatives to the *patotas*. He infiltrated the ranks of the women who came to be called 'The Mothers of the Plaza de Mayo,' the headscarved women who paraded silently in front of the junta's pink palace with the names of missing loved ones on boards hanging from their necks. These women were the true heroines of the Dirty War, defying truncheons and tear-gas to stage their weekly vigil, a vigil that played a powerful role in bringing the world's atten-

'WHEN ELECTRIC SHOCKS ARE APPLIED, ALL THAT A MAN FEELS IS THAT THEY'RE RIPPING HIS FLESH APART. AND HE HOWLS.'

THESE WOMEN WERE THE TRUE HEROINES OF THE DIRTY WAR, DEFYING TRUNCHEONE AND TEAR GAS TO STAGE THEIR WEEKLY VIGIL IN DEFIANCE OF THE JUNTA

THE MAN SPENDS DAYS CONFINED IN A CELL WITHOUT WINDOWS, WITHOUT LIGHT.

Opposite, top: ***A woman weeps at a 'No-Name' cemetery where thousands of Argentinians were dumped in unmarked graves after their murder by the junta.***

Opposite, below: ***The baby Clara Anahi Mariani disappeared after her parents were murdered. This baby was either abducted or killed by the junta.***

Left: ***The Mothers grew bolder and bolder. They knew they had to attract world attention to their plight if they were to defeat the regime.***

tion to the mass killings taking place in what the West had long regarded as the most 'civilised' of the South American nations. However, when the women's ranks were depleted by arrests, when their homes were raided or set on fire, when more members of their family disappeared, Gustavo Nino was always there to comfort them, never letting on that he had been the one who fed the damning information about their families back to his colleagues,

Above: ***After the junta fell, Argentinians began to dig up the unmarked graves.***

Opposite, top: ***The military roll their weapons through Buenos Aires.***

Opposite, below: ***Soldiers were seen as heroes before the ignoble Dirty War.***

who were waiting with the whips and the electric cattle prods and the flames.

For a time Astiz also worked out of his government's naval bureau in Paris, where he spied on exiled Argentinian human rights groups. After he was rumbled in Paris he headed for South Africa on a naval posting, but was hounded out of the country in 1981 when journalists learned of his unsavoury work at the Mechanics School. His superiors decided to pack him off to the war against Britain in the Falkland Islands in 1982.

THE TORTURER IS FREED

Astiz was captured by Royal Marines and when his name appeared in British newspapers, alarm bells began to ring in the capitals of the world. There were calls for his blood from Stockholm to Paris to the capital of his homeland, where thousands had a righteous claim on his murdering hide. But, under the terms of the Geneva Convention, Astiz was a prisoner-of-war and could not be handed over to foreign powers who suspected him of domestic crimes. He returned home after the war.

In Argentina, the following year, Raul Alfonsin was sworn in as the democratic president, the forty-first in the nation's history. His mandate was not only to steer the country towards democratic reforms, but also to exorcise the evil perpetrated upon his people by the junta. Some of the guilty men were brought to trial – including the suave torturer, Astiz. But he was never punished, never served time in a prison. At his pre-trial hearing his lawyers refused to admit that he had abducted and killed Dagmar – but in a supreme Orwellian twist said that if he had, it did not matter, because he was operating in a 'war time' situation. The military really did believe they were at war with their own people. He is now free in Argentina, a forty-two-year-old man with a wicked past but not a troubled conscience.

A commission was established after the war by the Alfonsin government to probe the terror. It found that the 'final purpose' of the terror was to exterminate the detainees and disfigure the bodies, so they could never be identified. The commission found no common factor to link the victims – they came from every level of

Argentinian society. Almost nine thousand of 'the disappeared' have never been found, despite the fact that more than sixty per cent of those seized were abducted in front of witnesses in public places. Three hundred and forty torture centres were unearthed – centres which, according to the junta, never existed. The commission produced a report fifty thousand pages long but the government failed to bring any of these state murderers to account.

Democracy now rules in Argentina, the dark days of 'The Process' are over. But the men in the olive green uniforms with the dark glasses are still there, lurking, waiting their next chance. Hebe Bonafini hopes they stay hidden. She was one of the founding members of the Mothers of the Plaza de Mayo and lost two sons and a daughter-in-law in thc terror. She said: 'The military went to war against people who spoke their own tongue. They never got the right ones anyway, just children, really, no one who was ever a threat. What happened to us must serve as a warning to all people all the time. It can happen anywhere you know, making people disappear. That is the tragedy of it. It can happen to anyone...'.

MAJOR PEIPER
Slaughter in the Snow

Adolf Hitler sneered at the traditions of war and even the most gallant German soldier was corrupted by him, but the heartless massacre of unarmed prisoners-of-war, left to die in the snow, will forever stain the honour of the German army.

By December, 1944, Adolf Hitler had lost his war in Europe but he refused to believe the truth. As the Russians advanced on Germany from the east, determined to vanquish the Germans and punish them for the cruel campaigns of the SS and Gestapo against their people, the Führer concocted one last-gasp scheme aimed at staving off defeat. He underestimated the Russians, and concentrated on the Western Front for he was convinced he could alter the course of the War by smashing the American and British advance. Operating from his 'Wolf's Lair' redoubt in Rastenburg, East Prussia, he was certain that by depriving the advancing armies in Belgium and France of their biggest and most vital supply port – Antwerp – he could slow down the advance, split the armies, starve them into submission, sue for peace and then turn every remaining piece of armour, every aircraft, artillery piece and his men against the Reds.

Any general in the German High Command, who was not a lickspittle or a flunky tried to dissuade Hitler from his scheme. At a time when reserves of men and material should have been preciously conserved, he wanted to waste them on a final, futile mission that everyone else knew would end in failure.

It not only ended in failure, it ended in dishonour as well. A renegade unit of SS troopers forever stained their gallant battle honours with the brutal, cold-blooded slaying of one hundred American troops. They were butchered in the snow, cut down by heavy machine-gun fire under a battle-group commanded by SS Major Joachim Peiper, and their bodies left to be covered by fresh snowfalls. For the Americans, who had seen SS brutality when they had liberated French towns and Nazi labour camps, the massacre made them fight even harder, made them more determined than ever to finish the War and settle the final score with Hitler once and for all. This massacre of one hundred soldiers, in the snow around the Belgian town of Malmedy, was a spur to the American troops in a way that no general's speech or extra training could ever have given them. The Battle of the Bulge in general – and the massacre at Malmedy in particular – served to hasten Fuhrer Adolf Hitler's demise.

THE REICH'S REMAINING HOPE

The German offensive was launched amid great secrecy on 16 December, 1944, in the mountainous, foggy region of the Ardennes Forest in Belgium. General Gerd von Runstedt, acting on Hitler's orders, had gathered together as many serviceable tanks, as much fuel, ammunition and heavy weaponry as he could, and forged them into a force on which every remaining hope of the dying Reich was pinned. There was no lacking the will to win – the Germans remained highly disciplined and supremely ordered – until the very end. But they were exhausted; morale was low.

THERE WAS NO LACKING THE WILL TO WIN – THE GERMANS REMAINED HIGHLY DISCIPLINED AND SUPREMELY ORDERED – UNTIL THE VERY END.

Opposite: ***Young American soldiers, including medics, were mown down in the snow. They were unarmed prisoners-of-war.***

Below: ***Adolf Hitler ignored his army officers and launched a futile attack against the Allies in 1944.***

IT WAS A GREAT BULGE IN THE ALLIED SECTOR – AND THE FIGHT TO REGAIN IT BECAME KNOWN AS THE BATTLE OF THE BULGE.

Hitler hoped to capitalize on the bad weather that shrouded this region in winter. He knew that the Allied air forces, which now roamed freely over Europe, would be grounded. Counting heavily on speed and surprise, he expected his armoured SS units – SS because he no longer had complete faith in the army, riddled with so many officers involved in the July 1944 plot that almost claimed his life – to be in Antwerp in a week. He put four armoured divisions of the SS Sixth Army under the command of his old pal Josef Dietrich at the spearhead of this important operation codenamed Autumn Mists.

Another specialist task, fiendishly concocted by Hitler who was forever pushing back the frontiers of conduct in war, was given to his master commando, Otto Skorzeny. Skorzeny, who had rescued Hitler's ally Mussolini in a daring glider operation on a mountaintop the previous year, was instructed to equip three thousand troops with American uniforms and put them behind American lines, thus causing confusion and chaos.

By the time the operation was launched von Rundstedt had scraped together a remarkable force from a nation that had lost nearly four million men since the start of the War. There were thirty divisions, t two thousand three hundred tanks, fifty self-propelled assault guns, and, miraculously, half of the three thousand combat aircraft promised by the chief of the Luftwaffe, Hermann Goering.

When the blow fell on the Allied lines it was shattering. Quite simply, complacent intelligence services of both the American and British armies had totally underestimated the reserves and willpower of the enemy facing them. The bad weather had, in fact, grounded Allied air operations, and would continue to do so for the next eight days. The sound of the German preparations for the commencement of the attack was drowned out by the relentless roar of V-1 rockets fired on Antwerp and the city of Liege. At 5.30am two thousand German heavy guns opened up with a storm of fire and steel on the Allied lines.

SS troops penetrated six miles of the line within hours at five different points. It was a great Bulge in the Allied sector – and the fight to regain it became known as the Battle of the Bulge. Hitler chose his élite Black Guard to spearhead the operation to spite the army officer corps. Of all the SS units thrown into the cauldron, none was braver or more decorated than the division which bore the Führer's name – the 1st SS Panzer Division *Liebstandarte* – 'Life

Above: ***This Ardennes landscape shows the harsh weather conditions in Europe when the Allies determined to crush the Germans.***

Guard' – Adolf Hitler. And commanding one battle group was the man whose name would always be linked to the infamous incident known as the Malmedy Massacre – Colonel Joachim Peiper.

Peiper was the epitome of gallant German manhood that Hitler adored. At twenty-nine, he was handsome, smart, fluent in three languages, supremely courageous and, unlike many fervent officers, had never joined the Nazi party. He was also possessed of a sparkling sense of humour, another trait uncommon among his officer comrades. By the time his Panzers shattered the American front line in the Ardennes, Peiper was known personally to his Führer. He had served with incredible bravery in the campaigns in Russia and had developed a reputation as a commando who knew when to obey orders and when to break them.

Among his men he was revered as a 'soldier's soldier' who did not go medal-hunting for the sake of it, although his exploits served to reward him with the Knight's Cross, Germany's highest battlefield honour. And he never left a wounded comrade in the field to be captured by the enemy if he could avoid it. Under Dietrich's command he was heading for Antwerp... but he doubted if he would ever reach it. Peiper rationalized that if he managed at least to reach the heights over the Meuse River he would have done his duty.

Like all SS formations at this stage of the war, with Germany having suffered over three million dead at the front, the once-strict Adolf Hitler division which once had not allowed foreigners to serve, had been forced to water-down its entry qualifications. *Volkdeutsche*, or ethnic Germans in conquered lands, were absorbed to fill the gaps in the ranks, along with other more racially-dubious candidates that would not have been given a second glance during the heady days of victory. Belgians, Rumanians, Dutchmen, Lithuanians – the turncoat youth of Europe were now being led by Joachim Peiper in this last-chance crusade against the allies.

PEIPER WAS REVERED AS A 'SOLDIER'S SOLDIER', WHO DID NOT GO MEDAL HUNTING ... AND NEVER LEFT A WOUNDED COMRADE TO BE CAPTURED BY THE ENEMY.

ADVANCE ON ANTWERP

Peiper commanded five thousand men with a formidable array of Tiger, Royal Tiger and Panther tanks, backed up with anti-aircraft units, self-propelled guns and heavy artillery. His job was to punch a hole in the line and race onwards to seize the Meuse bridgeheads – vital strategically if the mass of German armour was to cross the river to advance on Antwerp.

The initial hours went better than expected, the American line shattered, their mighty air armadas grounded. Panic swept

Below: ***Joachim Peiper was a brave soldier who had proved himself on the eastern front. Here, he leans over a jeep near Malmedy, the place where he lost his military honour.***

Above: ***Passing through woods infested with enemy snipers, weary troops dragged their equipment on sledges.***

the front as the battle-hardened *Liebstandarte* troops proved more than a match for the boys from Nebraska, Omaha and New York. But soon logisitical problems – problems that Peiper knew would make or break the operation – began to pile up. For one thing, he had been told to seize the bridgeheads although the high command knew full well he did not have enough fuel for such a venture. And, if the weather broke, at any time, his armour would be smashed on the ground by tank-busting fighters. Supply trains got lost or were held up at choked railway junctions and a fourth problem was the countryside; thick woods, and narrow medieval streets in the villages which were not easily navigated by seventy-ton metal monsters. Soon the advance momentum was lost.

HOPELESS TANGLE OF CONFUSION

In the fog of war – aided in part by the confusion created by Skorzeny's American-dressed commando squads – US units found themselves in a hopeless tangle of confusion and disorder the day following the initial assault. One such unit was the 285th Field Artillery Observation Battalion, a relatively inexperienced cadre of men composed mostly of teenagers who knew the business end of a rifle from its stock, but little else. Heading towards the Belgian town of Ligneuville, at a place called the Baugnez crossroads, the unit was trying desperately to link up with the US 7th Armoured Division which it believed had headed in the direction of Viesalm. But the 285th battalion was lost.

The company halted opposite the Bodarwe Café, where an officer enquired of the surly inhabitants if they were headed

Right: ***The snow rendered motor vehicles useless. Mules, the traditional heavy transport of war, were brought into the War in 1944.***

in the right direction because many road signs had been switched or simply torn down by Skorzeny's men. But these folk were not the welcoming oppressed villagers that had greeted the Allied advance throughout western Europe. Many of these 'border people' were fiercely pro-German, a traditional alliance that had been forged throughout centuries of shifting frontiers but unchanging causes and aims. The American was met with a mute shrug of the shoulders from the people inside.

As he went out to get his column moving again, the tanks of Kampfgruppe Peiper appeared like black beetles on the horizon. One of the beetles, a half-tracked armoured vehicle barked and a split second later the lead Jeep in the American column vanished in a flash of orange flame and black smoke. Then all the guns of the panzers opened up, one by one, as they crested the ridge and began their clanking crawl towards the scene of chaos and murder before them. The surprised and frightened American soldiers dived for cover in ditches, in a nearby barn, behind haystacks and even in a garden hedge. As soon as the German tanks were upon the shattered column, the cobbled road rang with the metallic clatter of dropped weapons as the Americans raised their hands in surrender and turned themselves over to their S.S. captors.

The Germans rounded the captured men up, frisked them for concealed weapons and pushed the prisoners into a field next to the crossroads. Peiper arrived on the scene, a Schmeisser machine pistol slung over his right shoulder. He ordered several of his men to stand guard on the captured 'Amis' then moved his other men off.

MENACE HUNG HEAVY IN THE AIR

Several of the prisoners began to have doubts for their safety. The guards seemed surly, angry, almost eager for an excuse, perhaps an escape attempt that allowed them to shoot. In the town of Bullingen, which the Germans had just left, they had captured one hundred American prisoners-of-war. Three had broken out, killing an S.S. guard by slitting his throat from ear to ear. Little wonder that a sinister menace hung heavy in that misty, damp air on the afternoon of 17 December, 1944.

'MACHEN ALLE KAPUT,' A VOICE WAS HEARD TO YELL ABOVE THE RACKET OF THE GUNS. 'KILL THEM ALL!'

The Americans sat and smoked in the snow-covered fields, watching glumly as prodigious amounts of enemy armour snaked and struggled to manouvre the tight crossroads along the road to Ligneuville, the route they had intended to take before they were ambushed. Young 2nd Liutenant Virgil Larry felt his throat going dry, as he gazed into the hard-eyes of the young stormtroopers, intoxicated with the flush of their small victory, as they sat atop their mighty panzers. He began to wonder what was going to happen to him and his company. At one point a massive self-propelled 88mm gun stopped in its tracks and traversed its menacing barrel directly at the American prisoners sitting quietly in the snow. But an angry German sergeant ordered it to move on with a curse.

Above: ***The field of slaughter in Malmedy. Those investigating dishonourable behaviour in the German unit marked the bodies of the murdered Americans with numbers.***

Then Peiper himself showed up again, riding on top of a King Tiger tank. With a smile and a wave he yelled out in perfect English: 'See you in Tipperary boys!' and was gone as the Tiger accelerated with a puff of blue diesel smoke belching from its twin rear exhausts. Finally, two armoured vehicles swung around the tight bend at the crossroads and stopped. Rumanian-born Georg Fleps, private first class, a member of the elite German division that would

Below: *Facing the Allies were German veterans of the Russian Front (top picture) The Americans (lower picture) were not daunted. They knew they were on the road to victory.*

have sneered at him in 1940, unbuttoned his holster, withdrew a Luger pistol and jumped to the ground. Walking like a gunslinger, he moved close to the massed ranks of the defenceless prisoners, raised his weapon and fired. An American dropped. He fired again and another dropped. Then the air was rent with the noise of automatic weapons as the heavy machine guns on the armoured vehicles barked in unison and the Americans were

mown down like corn under the relentless onslaught of a combine harvester. '*Machen alle kaput*,' a voice was heard to yell above the racket of the guns. 'Kill them all!'

Virgil Lary saw his driver drop dead, heard the shouts of an officer telling the men to 'stand fast' before he too was shot through the throat and killed. Homer Ford, a military policeman who survived the shooting, later said: 'Men were lying around moaning and crying. I dived under a body and feigned death. The shooting kept going on and on and I felt the blood of one of my buddies running over me.

'Soon the shooting stopped and I heard the Germans coming over. They would say: "Is he breathing?" and would either shoot or hit them with the butt of their guns. The closest they came to me was about ten feet. After they fired at us, I lay stretched out with my hands out and I could feel my blood oozing. I had been hit. I was lying in the snow, and I got wet and started to shiver, and I was afraid they would see me shivering, but they didn't. I had my head down and they couldn't see, but they were walking around the whole bunch and then they went over toward the road junction. I heard them shoot their pistols right next to me. I could hear them pull the trigger back and then the click. The men were moaning and taking on something terrible. I also heard the rifle butts hit guys' heads and then a terrible squishing sound.'

Samuel Dobyns, a medical orderly who had been recommended for a gallantry award, was one of the unit's few veterans who had been in Europe since D-Day in June. He was lying under the bodies, feigning death like Ford, when he heard the shooting stop and the single pistol shots which indicated that his comrades were being despatched with bullets in the head.

'I didn't want to die like a rabbit,' he said. 'I saw some woods off to the left and suddenly decided to make a run for it. I hadn't got more than twenty yards when I heard a heavy machine gun open up. I felt the slugs rip into me. I took four bullets, I later learned, and my clothes had been shredded by a further eight slugs. I heard Germans coming towards me, their boots crunching in the snow, and I knew they were going to finish me off. But they must have figured I was already dead. They turned around. I saw three or four Germans shoot wounded men who were crying for help. I thought I was the only one left alive.'

SHALL WE MAKE A RUN FOR IT?

Virgil Lary also survived and testified after the war at the trial of the killers: 'After the first machine guns fired, men fell dead and wounded all around me. The firing lasted for about three minutes, maybe a little longer. A man came by me as I lay feigning death and I heard a pistol shot nearby. Then I heard the sound of a new clip being inserted in a pistol and the individual passed me. I heard someone say to someone else: "Have they killed you yet?" He replied: "No not yet... but if the bastards are going to kill me I wish they would come back and get it over with." A bullet had severed my toes and I was in extreme pain and frozen from head to foot. Here and there I heard more raised voices: "Have they gone?" "What shall we do?"

"Is it safe?" "Shall we make a run for it?" Suddenly about fifteen of us decided to make a break for it. We had moved a few yards when rifles cracked, then a machine gun. I managed to clamber over a fence into a wood and ran along a dirt road until I came to a tumbledown shed. There were bundles of sticks inside and I pulled these all over myself. I waited.'

DRUNK WITH BLOOD

A few wounded men managed to crawl across the road to houses of local farmers as the '*Blustrausch*' – 'intoxication of the blood' – continued. But they were mown down before they entered, their bodies mangled by the tracks of the tanks and armoured vehicles of Peiper's rearguard that were now racing to catch up with the forward columns on the road to Ligneuville. Other Americans made it into the Bodarwe Café, but were flushed out by Germans who set it ablaze with flame-throwers. As they ran into the streets with their hands raised high they were mown down by the maddened German soldiers.

Soon silence settled on the field and the SS were gone. All that could be heard as dusk fell were the moans of the wounded and the dying, like the lowing of cattle. It was the most hideous crime ever visited upon American troops in the European theatre of war – one hundred men dead, forty-one alive, many seriously wounded. Soon the Germans in the front line would face the angry retribution of the US forces when they tried to surrender and found their enemy distinctly without mercy.

Word of the massacre sread faster than the bubonic plague through a medieval city. American units in their foxholds that night or billeted in girls' schools and town halls felt a bitterness welling inside them, a determination that turned them from raw troops into that most lethal of battlefield opponents – vengeful soldiers fighting for a cause; in this case, revenge for their murdered comrades. Hal Boyle and Jack Belden of 'Time Magazine' were allowed by the army brass into the crossroads, near the town of Malmedy, to photograph and record what the Germans had done that afternoon. One of the first people they interviewed was Lt Lary who had hobbled painfully from his hiding place. He shook his dismembered toes from his boot, along with the bullet that had severed them, and sobbed: 'We didn't stand a goddamned chance... We just didn't have a chance.' When the story reached the front page of the 'Stars and Stripes', the troops' newspaper, the 328th Infantry Regiment, in the thick of the fighting, received a written order: 'No SS troops or paratroopers will be taken prisoner, but will be shot on sight.'

Peiper's advance, and that of the rest of the German attacking force, ground to a halt before the Meuse eight days later. The weather cleared, the Allied air forces pounded the tanks and guns of the Germans into scrap metal and the final attempt by Hitler to hold Europe ended in defeated. Peiper retreated with his men... determined that no comrades should fall into enemy hands for as long as he led and controlled his men.

In the days after the massacre, but before the German surrender, the Judge Advocate's branch of the US army formed a special staff to collect evidence against the murderers at Malmedy. Peiper was captured defending Vienna at the end of the War, when he was an assistant divisional commander. He would pay the price for the crimes of his men at Malmedy, regardless of who had given the orders to open fire. With eight hundred survivors of his unit he was interrogated. Eventually he, the commanding SS General of the operation, Sepp Dietrich and seventy-three others, including

Below: ***A captured SS trooper was shown more mercy than was given to GIs caught at Malmedy.***

"HAVE THEY GONE?" "WHAT SHALL WE DO?" "IS IT SAFE?" "SHALL WE MAKE A RUN FOR IT?"

Above: ***The relief of Bastogne, the 'Bastion of the Battered Bastards', spelt the end of the German offensive – and the beginning of the Allied hunt for those responsible for the murders of GIs at Malmedy.***

the Romanian gunslinger who had fired the first shots into the unarmed American soldiers, stood trial.

The trial took place in Dachau, a fitting setting for retribution, for it was the site of the first concentration camp founded by the Nazis. The trial opened on 16 May, 1946, with chief prosecutor Lt Colonel Burton Ellis saying: 'The troops of the *Liebstabdarte* Adolf Hitler were told to excel in the killing of prisoners-of-war as in fighting. Others were told to make plenty of *rabbatz,* which in SS parlance means to have plenty of fun killing everything that comes in sight. Each defendant was a cog in a giant slaughter machine.'

Several of the prosecution witnesses were German soldiers themselves, sickened by what had taken place at the crossroads near Malmedy. Four enlisted men testified that Peiper had told them to 'give no quarter' in the battle and 'take no prisoners.' Corporal Ernst Kohler told the tribunal: 'We were told to remember the women and children of Germany killed in Allied air attacks and to take no prisoners, nor to show mercy to Belgian civilians.' Lt Heinz Tomhardt said: 'I told my men not to take prisoners.' So the Americans were killed.

There was gripping evidence at the trial from the survivors, men like Lary and Dobyns, who confronted Georg Fleps, the man who had first opened fire, and they said: 'This is the man who opened fire into unarmed prisoners-of-war.' As evidence piled on evidence it became clear that Peiper and his men were guilty. Peiper said that he had given no orders for the massacre. Dietrich said that he too had not passed down orders for prisoners to be murdered. But on 16 July, 1946, the dreadful words '*Tod durch erhangen*' – death by hanging – fell upon the ears of the once-gallant soldier, Joachim Peiper. Dietrich was also given the death sentence as were forty-two other German soldiers.

JUSTICE HAD NOT SERVED THE DEAD OF MALMEDY WELL.

In the end, none was executed. An Atlanta lawyer, William Meade Everett, who had been appointed defence counsel for the Germans at their trial, uncovered evidence that several German confessions of guilt had been extracted by the Americans using the methods that they had gone to war to abolish – namely torture and beatings. Burning matches were inserted under the fingernails of imprisoned SS troopers; several jaws were broken and men burned with cigarettes. It was shameful conduct, worthy of the Gestapo that they had defeated, not officers and men of the US army. Such charges sorely diminished the integrity of the tribunal and Everett, a lawyer with a keen sense of right and wrong, plunged thousands of dollars of his own money into having the cases re-opened.

On 29 July, 1948, a Senate Army Services Commission in Washington was empanelled to review the cases. By 1951 all the death sentences had been commuted and in 1958 Dietrich and Peiper were the last to be released. Justice had not served the dead of Malmedy well.

Joachim Peiper became the butt of many dishonourable accusations, but it seems clear that he was not tainted with any other acts of atrocity during the course of the War. He refused to talk about the old days, and explained his feelings: 'I am sitting on a powder keg. One day someone will come along with another accusation and the powder keg will explode. I'm a fatalist. The world has branded me and my men the scum of the earth. And no one will be able to clear up the Malmedy mess now. Too many lies have been told about it.'

And certainly, the truth died along with those brave men in the pasture next to the Baugnez Crossroads all those years ago.